*Global Society and International Relations*

# Global Society
## *and*
# International Relations

### Sociological Concepts
### and Political Perspectives

MARTIN SHAW

Polity Press

First published in 1994 by Polity Press in association with Blackwell
Publishers.

Editorial office:
Polity Press
65 Bridge Street
Cambridge CB2 1UR, UK

Marketing and production:
Blackwell Publishers
108 Cowley Road
Oxford OX4 1JF, UK

238 Main Street
Cambridge, MA 02142, USA

ISBN 0 7456 1211 3
ISBN 0 7456 1212 1 (pbk)

A CIP catalogue record for this book is available
from the British Library and from the Library of Congress.

Typeset in 11 on 13pt Sabon
by Photoprint, Torquay, S. Devon
Printed in Great Britain by Hartnolls Ltd, Bodmin, Cornwall

This book is printed on acid-free paper.

# Contents

# Acknowledgements

This book has been written over a period of engagement with international relations, stimulated by my involvement from 1989 to 1992 as Director of the Centre for Security Studies (formerly Defence and Disarmament Studies) at the University of Hull. I owe a particular debt to my then colleague, Nick Wheeler (now at Aberystwyth), for his encouragement, friendly criticism and generous sharing of ideas. I must also thank my MA students in security studies, on whom I have tried out many of the ideas developed here.

Earlier versions of several of the chapters have appeared as follows: Chapter 2, 'War and the Nation-State in Social Theory', in David Held and John Thompson, eds, *Social Theory of Modern Societies: Anthony Giddens and his Critics*, Cambridge: Cambridge University Press, 1989; Chapter 3, 'State Theory and the Post-Cold War World', in Michael Banks and Martin Shaw, eds, *State and Society in International Relations*, Hemel Hempstead: Harvester-Wheatsheaf, 1991, pp. 1–24; Chapter 4, as ' "There is No Such Thing as Society": Beyond Individualism and Statism in International Security Studies', in *Review of International Studies*, 19, 2, 1993, pp. 159–76; Chapter 5, as 'Global Society and Global Responsibility: the Theoretical, Analytical and Practical Limits of International Society', in *Millennium: Journal of Inter-*

*national Studies*, 21, 3, 1992–3, pp. 421–34; and Chapter 6, as *War is Over? The Left and the New World Order*, as a Democratic Left Discussion Paper, London, 1992. I am grateful to the editors and publishers of the original versions for their permission to republish.

I also wish to thank Barry Buzan and Ken Booth for their comments on earlier versions of Chapter 4; Rosemary Bechler for her support in publishing and stimulating discussion of *War is Over?*; Steve Platt, editor of *New Statesman and Society*, for encouraging me to write the article on the politics of military intervention, 'Grasping the Nettle' (15 January 1993), in which some of the ideas of the final chapter were first aired; and John Westergaard, President of the British Sociological Association, for inviting me to contribute to his 1993 Presidential Symposium on 'New Directions in Sociology'. Some of the ideas in Chapter 1 were first presented there.

# PART ONE

# Introduction

*One*

# The Theoretical Challenge of Global Society

As the twentieth century draws to its close, we are becoming aware of historic transformations of human society. The changes seem, indeed, truly millennial in their implications. For the first time since human beings inhabited this earth, it is possible to describe comprehensive networks of social relationships which include all people. We have not just some global connections – these have been developing for centuries – but the clear outlines of a global society. We have a global economic system, with production and markets coordinated on a world scale; elements of a global culture and worldwide networks of communication; globally vibrant political ideas and the possibility of coordinated political action. With the end of the Cold War, moreover, the international institutions which were seemingly still-born in 1945 are beginning to develop – albeit inadequately – as instruments of global order.

The emergence of global society is, however, beset by contradictions. Indeed one of the principal ways in which we can identify a global society is by the development of global crises. It is our common experience of fundamental disturbances, and the need to shape common responses, which is helping to bring global society into being. These crises are experienced at every level of social relations. They are socio-economic – as in the re-emergence of cyclical crises of the capitalist economy, which produce recessions now increasingly experienced in every corner of the globe. They are environmental – as in the production by global industry of harmful climatic effects which are felt everywhere, and are even seen as planetary phenomena. They are especially political – manifested in a unique turbulence of inter-state relations and instability of state structures, leading to new forms of war at civil as well as inter-state levels.

Global crises matter not merely because of their widespread harmful effects to human beings – poverty and unemployment, pollution and drought, dispossession and genocide. They are important too because it is through such crises that we can increasingly identify global society and the development of its institutions. Through an understanding of crises we can begin to grasp the forms which global society is taking and the processes transforming it in the present historical period.

Many global crises, and most obviously political crises, are often understood as international crises, that is, as crises of the inter-state system. Certainly, global crises of all kinds manifest themselves as international crises, but it is the argument of this book that such an understanding is limited, and in a certain sense superficial. Socio-economic, environmental and even political crises arise from a complex network of causes in worldwide social relations. They are commonly expressed within inter-state relationships because these are foremost among the institutional forms of world society. To consider them primarily as international phenomena is, however, to miss their complex causality and ramifications.

This book is concerned with global social developments, therefore, in a way which fundamentally challenges the common approach from the field of international relations. The aim of the book is to reconceptualize this field from the point of view of sociology in general, and the sociology of globalization in particular. Later chapters lay out, critically, some of the perspectives from sociology on the subject of nation-states, which are relevant to the understanding of international politics, together with detailed critiques of major concepts and perspectives in international relations. They also outline an alternative approach to understanding current global crises, together with a sociologically informed political approach to them.

In this chapter, however, the aim is to develop a sociological perspective on globalization and to suggest how inter-state relations might be conceptualized within this. We shall discuss some of the main approaches that are available within sociology, suggesting both their strengths and their weaknesses for an understanding of global processes, especially at the inter-state level.

## The world as a single society

The issue of globalization is a radical one for sociology as well as for international relations – and indeed for the social sciences as a whole. It challenges prevailing conceptions, especially many which are implicitly assumed in social theory and analysis, about the very nature of the social, the state and civil society.

The concept of society is fundamental to sociology, and its absence, weakness or unacceptable mutation, we shall see later in this book, is one of the definitive weaknesses of international relations. When Margaret Thatcher proclaimed 'There is no such thing as society', her statement was received as a challenge by every sociologist. And yet there can be no doubt that prevailing usages of 'society' are rendered highly problematic by the processes of globalization.

The term society is used in several senses. The most basic is as a generic term for social relations, which are the essential subject matter of sociology. In this sense, society is the totality or complex of social relations. Since social relations of all kinds are increasingly global, and all forms of social relations everywhere in the world are, at least in some indirect sense, bound into global networks, society in this sense is now necessarily global.

The term is also used, however, and perhaps even more

widely, in the sense of *a* society. The assumptions behind such usage is that there are relatively discrete complexes of social relations which can be distinguished from other such complexes and analysed in a largely self-sufficient manner. Note the qualifying adjectives, relatively and largely, for it is a long time since any known area of social life – probably not even the most recently 'discovered' peoples of New Guinea – could be said to be absolutely or wholly separated from wider frameworks of social relations.

There has always been a considerable paradox, and theoretical question-mark, behind most senses in which sociologists have talked of the existence of discrete societies. Such societies have always existed in relation to other societies and have been defined largely by such relationships. In modern times, moreover, societies have been defined by their state institutions and the specific forms of relationships between these. Hence, of course, the assumption by international theorists that inter-state relations can be regarded as largely autonomous from and analytically prior to social relations.

These considerations apply above all to national societies and the way in which they are related to nation-states. National societies, in the modern sense, depend on the existence of nation-states in a system of relations between states. National societies have been state-bounded segmentations of increasingly global social relations. Since there have always been, in modern times, international, transnational and even incipiently global relationships, such segmentations have always been quite arbitrary in some important respects. The ways in which description and analysis have tried to represent them as real – in a more or less absolute or fixed sense – has been patently false, and has reflected the incapacity of much sociology adequately to criticize national ideologies.

The same arguments apply, moreover, even to tribal societies. Such societies have generally existed, over thousands of years, only in relation to other similar societies. Societies, in the sense of discrete human communities, have only been formed through migration, differentiation and mutual contact. The circumstance of a wholly isolated society must be viewed, historically, as a limited exception in which a certain human group temporarily becomes isolated from others. In modern times, moreover, such societies have become increasingly defined by their contact with the Western nation-state system. Even the early anthropological studies, which attempted to define the pre-colonial forms of social relations, were in fact, as later critiques have established, manifestations of the colonial relationship between tribal societies and Western state-bounded societies.

There is a sense, then, in which the concept of discrete societies was always questionable, when not clearly identified as a partial abstraction from the global complex of social relations. A great deal of sociology has failed to enter the necessary qualifications and has accepted the national or state-bounded divisions as much more fixed and complete than they ever were. Such work has, of course, usually accepted the identity of nation and state, or national society and state, even where these ought to have been seen as problematic. (Thus most sociologists, before the 1970s, referred to British society without recognizing distinct Scottish or Welsh dimensions, and without acknowledging its atypicality in relation to the class of modern industrial capitalist societies.) Such work has tended to discuss the relations between national societies in terms of the comparative method, as though comparisons between societies were an adequate substitute for examining the common frameworks of relationships in which national entities were involved.

The national (and corresponding tribal) demarcation of societies worked, however, for a certain historical period. From the nineteenth-century heyday of the nation-state, in which classical sociology was largely developed, through the extreme national division of the world in the era of total war, the idea of national society corresponded to immediately comprehensible socio-political realities. The idea was still strong in the mid-twentieth-century 'post-war' condition, in which most modern sociology grew. Although many developments after 1945 were working to undermine this situation, the Cold War helped to freeze a certain conception of national society beyond the point at which it could really be sustained in its earlier form.

What is really new in the present situation, most clearly since the end of the Cold War, is that, although the idea of discrete national societies retains much resonance, its absolute supremacy among the ideas of society can no longer hold. This may seem a paradoxical assertion, since the strongest tendency of the years since 1989 has been the reassertion of nationalism. On all sides, people are breaking up multinational states into nation-states, and nation-states into miniature ethnically defined states. Socialism and communism seem to have given way, not to liberalism but to nationalism. And yet the desperation and violence of much of this return to the nation does not speak of an idea whose time has come, but of one which has to be upheld against all the odds.

The new nationalisms are not those of the classic, integrative nation-state, bonding disparate cultures into a single entity, but of the exclusive ethnic group, expelling all those who do not conform. The new nationalisms arise from the disintegration of nation-states and national societies. They reflect both historic pluralism and multi-ethnicity and new patterns formed as a result of recent migration and cultural change. Although ethnic identities seem the most powerful foci, they in fact exist alongside a powerful range of diverse, part-competing, part-overlapping forms of identity, centred on religion, gender, race, class, profession and lifestyle. The virulence of ethnic nationalism reflects its conflict not just with other nationalisms but with ideas of a plural society with multiple identities.

The idea of a national society in the old sense has thus declined as the ideas of a global society and of various more local forms of social identity have grown. The phenomenon of ethnic nationalism confirms rather than contradicts this development. The decline of national society brings to an end the idea of discrete segments in human society, or of discrete societies. It leaves us with the idea of a single global society, segmented in many different ways – not least by the system of nation-states and by national and ethnic identities – but in which no one form of differentiation is so dominant as to enable us to adopt it as a general principle of analysis. All discussion of society within particular regions, states or local communities, or within particular culturally defined limits, must be recognized as a relative abstraction from the global complex of social relations, and one which must ultimately be returned to an analysis of this whole.

## Integration in global society

To describe global social relations in terms of a society immediately raises critical issues about the meaning of the concept. Different schools of sociology have fought over it in the past, with clear lines of division, in a classic debate which is highly relevant to the current discussion. For some theorists, a society is characterized by normative consensus, reflected in commonly accepted institutions. For others, it is formed simply by the existence of networks of relationships, with mutual expectations, even if the commonality of values and norms among the members is highly limited. The mutual expectations may indeed be of sustained and systematic conflict over values as well as resources.

These divided notions of the meaning of a society are also prevalent but, as we shall see later in this book, largely unacknowledged and untheorized in the international relations debate. In this section, however, we shall explore the sociological meaning of global society, and try to illuminate the issues posed by the dual definitions of society which are on offer.

In order to utilize the dilemma constructively, it is important not to entrench ourselves in the polar positions of 'conflict' and 'consensus' which characterize textbook discussions in sociology. It may indeed be preferable, as a starting point, to examine the *de facto* patterns of social relations, and it is unjustifiable to assume the existence of *de jure* normative consensus as the foundation of society: to this extent the present writer shares the materialist view of the foundations of conflict. As David Lockwood argued, however, in a classic attempt to overcome the polarity, it may be more relevant to see these two approaches as indicating two distinctive dimensions of social cohesion, which can be characterized respectively as 'system' and 'social' integration.[1] The former concerns the extent to which a society's members are factually integrated in social relationships; the latter, the extent to which they are normatively integrated. Lockwood's argument suggests that these are not questions of definition, but empirical issues in the assessment of any given society.

Two versions of 'system' integration may be identified as structuring the sociological debate on globalization. Immanuel Wallerstein's 'world-system' approach analyses the world in terms of the development of global capitalism, in which the division between economic, political and social relationships is seen as artificial. For Wallerstein, globalization is the development of a unified world-system dominated – critics would say excessively – by the socio-economic relationships of capitalism.[2] Wallerstein has recently extended his analysis into the cultural dimension of the world-system, seeing this as dominated by a tension between universalism and particularism (in the form of racism-sexism).[3] This remains, however, a highly simplified view of global society, juxtaposing a one-dimensional view of culture and values with a similar perspective on market relationships.[4]

Anthony Giddens, on the other hand, has proposed a view of globalization which conceptualizes systemic arrangements as multiple and complex. In Giddens's view, modern society is dominated by knowledge-based abstract systems which co-ordinate human activity, and which enable as well as constrain individual action and choice. For Giddens, the globalization of abstract systems creates opportunities for individuals, as well as crises in which they have constantly to remake their own lives and identities.[5] It is clear from Giddens's view that the increasing integration of systems (plural) does not necessarily imply greater social integration on a global scale. On the contrary, the crises brought about by the failures of or contradictions between the various abstract systems could lead to greater problems of social integration.

Applying the distinction between system and social integration to the developing global society may, therefore, illuminate many of the issues which concern current analysis. Global society clearly exhibits growing system integration, above all at the level of socio-economic relations, but also in the development of cultural and political institutions. What is a great deal more problematic is the development of social integration in the value sense. How far has the growing integration of global systems been accompanied by a genuine emergence of consensus and normative integration? In so far as such developments are occurring, are they confined largely to state, corporate and intellectual elites, or do they involve larger sections, or even all the members of global society?

Merely to pose these questions is to underline how limited and fragmentary is the process of globalization. Clearly the emerging global society is divided by fractures of many kinds – of income, wealth and class; of knowledge and power; of gender, lifestyle and culture; and, of course, of nation, race and ethnicity. The obstacles to social integration (of the kind classically understood by sociologists) are so many that even a comprehensive description and analysis would actually be very difficult.

Does this mean that the concept of global society should be employed only in a factual and never in a normative sense? In reality such a division cannot be made, because the two dimensions actually concern aspects of the same relationships. Even global market relations and the most limited global coordination of production involve the growth of common expectations and ideas of social life. The global coordination of communications, even more obviously, diffuses ideas and values which become increasingly commonly held. The growth of global politics is not just the bringing of very diffuse interests into relations with one another; it also involves the development of a common language and values (of democracy, rights, nation, etc.) in which conflicts are articulated.

It is worth exploring further, therefore, what might be meant by asserting that the social or normative integration of global society is less developed than its systemic or factual integration. Essentially the proposition would seem to revolve around two main absences: of a developed and generally acknowledged central system of beliefs and values (such as have been attributed, often somewhat dubiously, to national societies); and of central institutions which clearly embody, uphold and enforce these beliefs and values, and which are in turn widely accepted in global society.

It is evidently correct to argue that global society, in its existing or likely future form, does not and will not possess either common beliefs and values, or common and accepted institutions, to even the problematic extent to which these have been attributed to national or tribal societies. Indeed it is difficult to argue that global society could ever possess these forms of cohesion in the same ways, or to the same degree, as these more limited societies. This is true because, however fast global integration proceeds, world society seems likely in the foreseeable future (centuries as well as decades) to remain divided between highly differentiated segments. The experience of society in complex multinational states has been that national, ethnic and other divisions remain powerful; it seems inconceivable that these will be less important on the much larger scale of global society, however much global institutions develop. The reverse is more likely to be true, as globalization sharpens existing differences.

Global social integration seems likely, therefore, to remain extremely problematic. Sociologists have, however, analysed cultural developments as one of the main forms of globaliz-ation, and such developments pose the issue of integration particularly sharply. A global culture which equates with national cultures may not exist, Featherstone argues, and alleged homogenizing processes ('theories which present cultural imperialism, Americanization and mass consumer culture as a proto-universal culture riding on the back of Western econ-omic and political domination') may have been exaggerated.

Nevertheless we can conceptualize global culture, 'in terms of the diversity, variety and richness of popular and local discourses', with an 'image of the globe as a single place, the generative frame of unity within which diversity can take place.'[6]

Anthony Smith, an authority on nationalism, reminds us that the development of global means of communication does not necessarily mean that a common content is shared in all societies.[7] On the contrary, national cultures may maintain or even increase their vibrancy in response to globalizing tendencies. However, a historical perspective such as that proposed by Roland Robertson suggests that the diffusion of nationalism can itself be seen as part of the process of globalization.[8] In his account, the standardization of the nation as the basis for society and state was a facet of the early stages of globalization. By implication, its continuing importance, on which Smith rightly insists, has nevertheless to be seen in the context of the current phase of globalization. Every nationalism is different, but all nationalisms use a common language and symbols – which are global currency. Nationalisms are, as Smith himself suggests, becoming hybrids, exchanging ideas with one another and with other elements in global political discourse. If nations are, in Anderson's term, imagined communities,[9] then one has to be aware of this worldwide intercourse which feeds the way in which nations are imagined.

This discussion suggests that the problem of socio-cultural integration in global society should not be conceptualized in one-dimensional terms. The idea of a simple homogenization is patently inadequate – although homogenizing processes certainly exist – but even diversity can be seen to have integrating aspects. We can, indeed, go further, and argue that the conflictual aspects of diversity, where cultural differentiation is linked to political conflict, can be seen under the rubric of global integration. Conflict sharpens awareness of mutual dependence and promotes the development of common responses and institutions for regulation, which in turn involve cultures of cooperation.

## Global culture, institutions and civil society

How then do we conceptualize global society? Does its analysis require entirely new concepts, or can we transfer the concepts with which sociologists have analysed national societies to a global level? We have looked at some of the issues which arise with the idea of society itself, but this is the most general (and often vague and implicit) of the major concepts. It is important to examine the more specific concepts which are widely used, in their theoretical contexts, in relation to some of the manifest dimensions of globalization.

The conceptualization of global society is not the novelty which it might appear at first glance. A central paradox of sociology is that, while most *analysis* assumes national societies, the major *theories* are centred on concepts which either implicitly or explicitly transcend national frameworks. Sociological analysis has most commonly been carried out at national or sub-national levels, and where it has advanced beyond these has been based on the comparison of national societies. Theory, on the other hand, has been based on paradigms such as that of industrial society and modernization, which has sat uneasily within national frameworks, and of the capitalist mode of production, which is explicitly transnational and incipiently global. The contradiction has tended to be resolved in practice by the domestication of concepts, as concepts such as class have been treated as appropriate to a national level and shorn of their potentially global significance. In part, of course, sociology has here reflected the real contradiction that, despite developing globalization, many levels of society remain linked to the nation-state.

For the purposes of understanding globalization, however, the important fact is that many sociological categories, commonly associated with national-level analysis, are already implicated in transnational or global theorization. The ideas of a global economy, global markets and a global socio-economic system are commonplace and already recognized in social science areas such as international political economy, which bridges economics and international relations. Within sociology, the concepts of capitalism as a mode of production and a social formation have given a more specific formulation to these same realities, even if the relations between national and global contexts have not always been adequately theorized.

The concept of the state is one which is most ambiguously situated in relation to the global problematic. On the one hand, much of the sociological and political-science literature about the state, especially but not exclusively from within the Marxist tradition, locates states far too narrowly in relation to social relations within national contexts. Much recent sociological writing, however – most notably the works of Giddens, Mann and Skocpol – has placed the dimensions of external state relations in general and military power in particular in a newly central place in our understanding of modern society. A new paradigm has become established in which *the* state is no longer the theoretical object, but has been displaced by the state-system in which the relations of states among one another are of critical importance.

Critics have pointed out the danger of simply shoring up the equally one-sided view of the realist school of international relations, and this is a real issue which is explored in later chapters of this book. From the point of view of global sociology, however, the emphasis on the state-system also has highly positive implications: it opens up the possibility of theorizing the relations between state–state and state–society relationships.

Another central concept which is implicated in this ambiguity is that of civil society. The idea of a complex of culture and institutions which mediates the relations of social groups to the state, and in which individual citizenship is grounded, would seem to be most clearly located in the national or domestic context and linked to the nation-state. With globalization, however, it is clear that economic, cultural and political relations develop rapidly independently of the relations between states. National civil societies cease to be self-sufficient, even in the partial sense in which they might previously have been said to have been. Individuals and groups within society begin to develop relationships with international (inter-state) institutions, mediated through cultural forms and institutions of civil society which have themselves developed beyond the national context. In this sense, even the concept of civil society which appears to be firmly located in the national setting now has to be, and can be, extended to the global level – although what precisely is implied here needs considerable explication.

Certain theoretical perspectives and debates have clearly played crucial roles in opening up the understanding of globalization. The concept of modernity has been central, and with it the debate about post-modernity, in clarifying the universalizing tendencies of modern social relations. The limited concept of the modern which is assumed by much post-modernist writing implies a connection between modernity and the nation-state, which is now being transcended. The more general concept of modernity advanced by critics of this view, such as Giddens, offers the alternative of viewing the nation-state as one partial, and historically limited, expression of modernity, but nevertheless one which continues to form part of current tensions. In either case, however, there is an agreement in seeing the contradictions between national and global forms as central to current trends in society.

This discussion leads to the conclusion that the theoretical perspectives and central concepts of sociology can be utilized in understanding global society, but that they cannot be uncritically transposed to this very different level. What is necessary is a process of theoretical transformation which takes account of the fundamental differences between global and national contexts, and understands the historical transformations of their relations which are taking place. To some extent, the theoretical changes are precisely what have been developing in the debate about modernity, in the new thinking about states and in the analysis of cultural change and communications over the last fifteen years. What has not yet been done, however, is systematically to bring together the central concepts in a way which enables us to conceptualize global society as a whole and the relations between its various components.

One of the problems is that to formulate the task in this way could lead to the dangers of the concepts of social system and social formation which have been well criticized in their Parsonian and Marxist versions. To emphasize the increasing reality of a society at the global level could be said to impose a false unity on very complex sets of relationships and to minimize the unevenness of unifying processes. More fundamentally, it could be seen as shifting the focus from processes and relationships to a more static concept of a social system. The critique of functionalism, levelled at Marxist accounts of the capitalist system as well as against post-war American theories, could easily be revived against any attempt to define global society as a closed and self-sufficient system.

Global society does not have to be defined, however, in this way. Global society, to put it at its strongest, is no more or less than the entire complex of social relations between human beings on a world scale. As such it is more complete and self-sufficient than just about any other society which has been or could be envisaged. It still represents a partial abstraction relative to the history of human societies, and relative to the natural and living world as a whole. It does not have to be seen as having needs (as in the original functionalist model), as being based on imperatives (such as capital accumulation in the Marxist account of capitalism) or as necessarily entailing a given set of functions and institutions. Its emergence and the social relations, systems and institutions within it can be described under the rubric of historical discontinuity and contingency rather than of functional or historical necessity.

While global society in this sense contains all social relations, not all relations are actually defined at a global level. Global society can also be seen, therefore, as the largest existing, and also the largest possible, framework or context of social relations, but not necessarily the immediately defining context of all social relations. As in all large-scale, complex societies there are many contexts in which relations can be defined, and most are not located in the largest or most general context. Crucial to understanding global society is to comprehend the changing contextualization of social relations, and one of the critical issues is to grasp the extent, forms and processes of globalization. Globalization, indeed, can be seen as the way in which social relations become defined by specifically global contexts.

Global society can be said to exist, in the sense that global relationships are sufficiently strong and established to be defined as the largest context of social relationships as a whole. In an equally if not more important sense, however, it can still be seen very much as an emergent reality. Obviously, the historical origins and phases of globalization are a very important question: Robertson traces it back to the mid-eighteenth century and, in its 'germinal phase', to the fifteenth century; no doubt even earlier antecedents could be found.[10] Even if globalization has been gathering momentum over recent centuries and (especially) decades, there are clearly important senses in which global society appears – by comparison with more restricted historical societies – to be in its early stages. There is, for example, no concept of deglobalization, which suggests that the momentum is still very much in one direction, even if the tensions in the process are of critical importance.

If global society is still emergent, then this should increase our caution over ascribing to it forms which have characterized previous societies, and draw our attention to its historically specific features. A fundamental feature of global society is the exceptional complexities of its segmentation and differentiation, which subsumes and transforms the complexity of the pre-existing civilizations and national and tribal societies while producing many more from the processes of globalization themselves. The form of global society is, for this reason, a standing reproach to any simple functionalism, since any attempt to identify institutions with functional prerequisites will immediately founder on the institutional complexity and diversity of global social arrangements and the unevenness of globalization. Likewise, although the existence of global production and markets may seem to indicate a plausible case for a Marxist approach ('world-system' or otherwise), this constitutes at best a partial case, since these forms have developed within a complexity and diversity of institutions and cultures which have many effects on them, and which cannot be explained by them.

Global society is best understood, therefore, as a diverse social universe in which the unifying forces of modern production, markets, communications and cultural and political modernization interact with many global, regional, national and local segmentations and differentiations. Global society should be understood not as a social system but as a field of social relations in which many specific systems have formed – some of them genuinely global, others incipiently so, and others still restricted to national or local contexts.

Given the segmentation of global society, many of its institutions take a qualitatively different form from those of other societies. The most evident difference between global and national societies is the lack of a centralized state. The contrast here is, however, a false one, since national societies in modern times exist only by virtue of three conditions: their dependence on particular states, these states' relationships with other states, and the segmentation of wider social relations in line with state divisions. These fundamental, structuring facts are overlooked in any comparison which takes national societies as a baseline for global society. We should consider national societies not as a general model, but as characterized by a historically specific relationship of state and society. This is not necessarily appropriate to Western societies at all historical stages, and may not apply to other societies (for example, tribal societies – however much some anthropologists have searched for comparable state institutions). This model of state and society cannot, by definition, be applied to global society since the latter constitutes the framework for the existence of this relationship in the national cases.

Where national societies have states, therefore, global society has a state system. We are so used to thinking of the society–state relationship in a one-to-one sense, in a which a single state constitutes the ultimate source of power and authority in a given society, that this concept of state power in global society may seem confusing. The familiar concept of one

society, one state is, however, a historically specific one, and
to generalize it, and expect any newly identified society to
conform to it by definition, is to be guilty of illegitimate
generalization.

Interestingly, international relations theorists have characterized the state system as an anarchic one, and in a well-known
work Hedley Bull defined 'international society' as an 'anarchic
society' comparable with 'primitive' stateless societies.[11] There
are problems, which are discussed later in this book, with this
concept of international as opposed to global society. In
particular, the definition of it as a 'society' of states to be
compared with societies composed of individual human beings
raises severe methodological problems. Nevertheless, the idea
that a society can be characterized by anarchic relations – that
is, by the absence of a clear central authority structure, and in
particular of a central state – is clearly valid.

Although we are used to the idea of a society in which
economic relations are anarchic (the essence of a market-based
economy), the idea of political anarchy is challenging. Yet
global society is a society in which anarchy prevails at both
these crucial levels of social organization. The economic system
of global society is at root that of the global market,
coordinating an enormously complex division of labour in the
production and exchange of commodities. The political system
of global society is basically that of the competitive international system of states, coordinating an equally complex
diversity of national-state politics. The global cultural system is
largely one of diverse, part-competing, part-overlapping, part-
distinctive, part-integrated national and sub-national cultures
organized around a wide range of principles.

The novel sense in which we talk of a global society at the
end of the twentieth century depends, however, on something
more than an awareness of these various forms of anarchy
(which have characterized the emerging global society for
decades if not centuries). Nor is it merely that, as a result of the
development of communications, we have a heightened awareness of the anarchic nature of our world. This is important, but
what is most significant is that as a result of this heightened

awareness we are beginning to experience transformations of systems, institutions and culture. Military, political, economic and cultural crises are increasingly defined as global crises; even relatively limited regional conflicts are seen as global issues. Global society is beginning to be more than the sum of its parts, or, to be more precise, more than a framework for the competition of its parts.

It is in this sense that we should view the development of specifically global institutions (as well as regional and other transnational institutions). The global economic system consists not merely of a global division of labour and global market exchanges, but increasingly also of a variety of global (and regional) economic institutions aiming to regulate these processes. Although such institutions – GATT, IMF, Group of 7, EC, etc. – are dominated by the major Western states, banks and other corporations, they are distinct from any specific state or private interests and operate effectively as global regulators.

The global political system, similarly, consists not merely of an ever-growing number of individual nation-states and alliances or groupings of states. Global (and regional) institutions – above all, with all its defects, the UN – play an increasingly critical role. No matter that such institutions are manipulated by the major Western powers, and that their actions – especially military intervention (as in the Gulf in 1990–1) or non-intervention (as in Bosnia in 1992–3) – depend largely on the interests and policies of these powers, and especially of the USA. These are the developing global political institutions, and not surprisingly they reflect the current realities of global politics.

The global cultural system likewise can be characterized by the growth of global and regional elements. Although no one should doubt the tenacity of particularistic ideas and identities, as of particular economic and political interests, the growth of a common culture is still very striking. It is not just, of course, that means of communication have been transformed and that global communications systems have developed, dominated like most other economic fields by Western corporations with global reach. Nor is it merely that the standard cultural commodities – images, ideas, information – of Hollywood and CNN are globally diffused. More important, although less easily summarized, are the ways that through these processes, intermeshing with economic and political globalization, people are coming to see their lives in terms of common expectations, values and goals. These cultural norms include ideas of standard of living, lifestyle, entitlements to welfare, citizenship rights, democracy, ethnic and linguistic rights, nationhood, gender equality, environmental quality, etc. Many of them have originated in the West but they are increasingly, despite huge differences in their meanings in different social contexts, parts of the ways of life and of political discourse across the world. In this sense, we can talk of the emergence of a global culture, and specifically of global political culture.

A vital issue here is whether we can posit the growth of a global civil society. The concept of civil society forms a pairing with that of the state. In a weak and inclusive sense, civil society denotes society as distinct from the state; in this sense, clearly we can talk of a global civil society, based on the emerging global economy and culture. In a stronger sense, however, writers such as Gramsci have seen civil society in terms of the way in which society outside the state organizes and represents itself, forming both a source of pressure on and, in a certain sense, an extension of the state. Civil society in this sense is constituted by its institutions – classically churches, press, parties, trade unions, etc., but in modern terms also including a variety of communications media and new (no longer directly class-based) social movements and campaigns. The institutions of civil society have historically been national and constituted by the relationship to the nation-state; indeed they may be said to be essential components of the nation. Civil society has been, almost by definition, national.

It is clear that this situation, too, has begun to change in a fundamental way. As an increasing number of issues are being posed in global terms, the common threads weaving together civil societies in many countries have grown ever stronger. Between Western societies, the creation of a common military system during the East–West conflict, and with it of a common economic space, has encouraged the linking of civil societies. Within Western Europe, especially, the development of the European Union at a state level has brought forward – however contradictorily, since there is also societal resistance to European unity – a greater convergence of civil society. Across the former communist world, the collapse of the system revealed the weakness of civil society; while one result is a resurgence of nationalism, there is also an unprecedented opening of civil society to the West. In the rest of the world, there is also a decline of ideas of a Third World, and with it of the programme of national economic independence. There is a greater worldwide recognition of global interdependence, which has been strengthened since 1989.

Does the global linking of civil society amount to the development of global civil society? Clearly such a development must be in its early stages, and yet there are reasons for saying that it has well begun. The growth of common expectations, values and goals – the beginnings of a common world culture and especially a political culture – is not simply reflected in parallel demands in individual nation-states. It is reflected in the growth of common expectations of the state system, with demands throughout the world for action by the 'international community', and in particular in new expectations of international institutions such as the UN. As suggested at the beginning of this chapter, global crises play a crucial role in forging the global consciousness which represents the awakening of a global civil society. At an institutional level, the responses are still weak, although non-governmental human rights, humanitarian aid and environmental agencies, developed from the West but with global reach, are important forms in the embryonic global civil society.

Civil society, we have noted, has always been seen as symbiotically linked with the state. Global civil society is coming into existence in an interdependent relationship with the state system, and especially with the developing international state institutions. The development of global civil society can best be understood in terms of a contradictory relationship with the state system. Civil society represents

social interests and principles which may well conflict with the
dominant interests in the state system. Just as national civil
societies may express ideologies which are in contradiction to
state interests, so global civil society, in so far as it is
constructed around ideas of human rights, for example, may
express ideologies which are formally upheld within the state
system, but whose consistent application is in contradiction
with dominant state interests. Global civil society thus constitutes a source of constant pressures on the state system,
although its development is in turn very much dependent on
developments in the state system.

National civil societies have gone hand in hand with national
identity as a dominant principle in people's identity-formation.
As we have noted, the overarching importance of national
identity has declined, although it remains a – perhaps the most
– powerful principle among many. The development of global
civil society raises the issue of how far global principles of
identity are now becoming important. Clearly important
groups in all parts of global society are beginning to see
membership of this society as a key identifier, alongside
nationality and other affiliations. In some parts of the world,
other forms of transnational identity are becoming more
important – Europeanism, for example, which fairly clearly has
close links to globalism, and Islam, which although universal in
form is (like most other traditional religions and political
ideologies) potentially antithetical to globalism in practice. The
strength of globalism and related transnational identifiers is a
key sociological test of the emergence of global civil society.


## Sociology, international relations and global society


The global society perspective which has been outlined in this
chapter constitutes a theoretical challenge to the social sciences
as a whole, and to sociology in particular. There is in fact a
dual challenge, the implications of which are pursued throughout this book. The challenge to sociology – and by extension to

most other social sciences, such as economics, politics, social geography and social history – is to move its level of theoretical and even more of analytical inquiry from the national to the global level, and to recast its categories explicitly in globalist terms.

The challenge to international relations, however, is of a different sort. International relations can be seen as the prime example of a field which is incipiently global, in that its *raison d'être* is to deal with relationships beyond the national level. The challenge to international relations is to move beyond the misplaced abstraction of state relations from the global whole. In the case of international relations, the movement to globalism is from a different starting point, and involves rather different sorts of transformation.

A major part of the paradox of international relations is that inter-state relations have developed further, with stronger institutionalization, than global economic, cultural or social developments. International relations seem therefore to possess a priority – analytical, if not real – over understanding the shifting sands of these other sorts of relationship in global society. International relations has been constructed, as a discipline, on this premise, but now finds it necessary to adjust to the fuller understanding of global society in its widest sense. How far, and how deep, the adjustment should go, is part of the question of this book.

Even deeper in the paradox, however, is that international relations theorists have always implicitly recognized the links between state and society. The very name *international* relations implies a concern with relations between nations rather than states. While its intention may be honourable, international relations is a misnomer in so far as the discipline has always really been about relations between states. Its practitioners have generally made the mistake of assuming that states represented nations, and that the interests of the latter are incorporated in the former. When we look at the nation as only one principle of social, cultural and political organization in an increasingly complex global society, the very foundations of the study of international relations are theoretically challenged. The relations between states may remain a legitimate focus of study, but its basis will be recast within a wider globalism.

In the remaining chapters of this book, these issues are pursued by means of engagements with recent major theoretical contributions in both sociology and international relations. We shall first examine the implications of rethinking the sociological theory of the state, looking at the movement beyond national or internalist conceptions to a focus on the state system. We shall then look at the ways in which state theory figures in international relations, and move from this to examine the problems of statist and nation-centred categories in international relations – both in general and in the current rethinking of the bases of security. We shall look at the particular theoretical difficulties of the concept of 'international society'. And, finally, we shall return to the globalist perspective in a more activist examination of its implications for global politics.

## NOTES

1   David Lockwood, 'Social integration and system integration'. In G. K. Zollschan and W. Hirsch, eds, *Explorations in Social Change*, New York: 1964; repr. in Lockwood, *Solidarity and Schism*, Oxford: Clarendon Press, 1992, pp. 399–412.
2   Immanuel Wallerstein, *The Modern World-System*, 3 vols, New York: Academic Press, 1974.
3   Wallerstein, 'Culture as the ideological battleground of the modern world-system'. In Mike Featherstone, ed., *Global Culture: Nationalism, Globalization and Modernity*, London: Sage, 1990, pp. 31–56.
4   See the comments of Roy Boyne, 'Culture and the world-system'. In Featherstone, *Global Culture*.
5   Anthony Giddens, *The Consequences of Modernity*, Cambridge: Polity, 1990, and *Modernity and Self-Identity*, Cambridge: Polity, 1991. These works are discussed more fully later in this book.

6 Mike Featherstone, 'Introduction'. *Global Culture*, p. 2.

7 Anthony D. Smith, 'Towards a global culture?' In Featherstone, ed., *Global Culture*, pp. 171–91.

8 Roland Robertson, 'Mapping the global condition'. In Robertson, *Globalization: Social Theory and Global Culture*, London: Sage, 1992, pp. 49–60; also in Featherstone, ed., *Global Culture*, pp. 15–30.

9 Benedict Anderson, *Imagined Communities*, London: Verso, 1979.

10 Robertson, 'Mapping the global condition'. In *Globalization*, pp. 58–9.

11 Hedley Bull, *The Anarchic Society*, London: Macmillan, 1977.

PART TWO

# State Theory: The Relevance of Sociology

# Two

# War and the Nation-State in Social Theory

At the centre of the new critical relationships between sociology and international relations has been the question of the state. The new sociological theory of the state, developed in the 1980s, placed the state in the context of the state system and thus opened up a dialogue with international theory.[1] Sociological accounts have been widely seen as making a significant contribution to discussion in international relations, although there has been no shortage of criticism either – often from those who feel that sociological writers have conceded too much to traditional international relations orthodoxy. One critic argues that 'current sociological theories of the state are increasingly approaching a more traditional view of the state – the state as actor model – precisely at a time when the theory of international relations is getting away from this idea and taking a more sociological form.'[2]

The most influential of all the new accounts of the state has been Anthony Giddens's analysis of the relationship between the pacification of societies through surveillance and the concentration of violence in the outward-pointing activities of nation-states.[3] In this chapter, we explore the social theory of the state largely through a critical examination of Giddens's account; in the following chapter, we look at state theory in the new context of international relations in the post-Cold War world. In both chapters we shall address the criticisms of recent sociological contributions from international theorists, while raising some critical questions of our own from a sociological standpoint, and examining the significance of these developments for a theory of global society.

## The problem of war and the theory of the state

At the centre of all the new sociological theorizing on the state has been a renewed sense of the importance of war. Here, the new school has been addressing a central issue of modern international relations which reverberates through the historical development of society, but which sociology has traditionally neglected. Giddens's work, in particular, defines warfare as one of the four major institutional clusters of modern society and one of two which are central to the state; the way in which warfare is dealt with is, therefore, of major significance.

The history of the twentieth century has often been written as that of a 'century of total war'.[4] Centuries are not, of course, socio-historical periods, but the idea of 'total war' expresses a dominant reality of the recent history of global society – from the 1890s to the 1950s, the period of the build up to, the fighting and the aftermath of the two World Wars. It can also be argued that one of the most important group of questions about late twentieth-century global society is whether and in what senses we have superseded, or can supersede, the period of total war.

In the history of twentieth-century social theory, however, war hardly figures. The major writers have continued the debates of nineteenth-century thinkers about industrialism and capitalism, recognizing war – if at all – as an event external to the main processes of social change.[5] The late twentieth-century boom in sociology, even radical and Marxist, has uncritically taken 1945 as the baseline of modernity, failing to reflect on the processes of war which determined this major rupture in social history.

This failure goes beyond sociology to encompass other disciplines and orientations in social science and the humanities. It is not a secondary or minor problem which can be met simply by partial adaptations of the social sciences, for example by developing a new sociology, geography or philosophy of war, however useful the contributions which these may make.[6] It is a central issue in the interpretation of global society, a key problem of social theory in general.

The virtual absence of the problem of war in any mainstream tradition of social thought has many ramifications. Its consequences are not limited to the evident weakness of the sociological contribution to problems of war and peace. Total war, in the earlier part of the twentieth century, was a fundamental process in the restructuring of state, economy and society. A social theory which has not grasped the nature and role of this mode of warfare historically is ill-equipped to deal with the effects which its mutation, in the current period, has on economic and social life. The profound transformations of economy, politics and culture in global society at the end of the twentieth century are explicable only against the backdrop of the changes in total war – which shaped the earlier 'post-war' world.

The re-emergence of war, war-preparation and militarism as sociological issues was partly a reflection of the new public awareness of these problems in the 1980s. The new sociology of war widened the focus from the sociology of the military, which until then was the only significant manifestation of these issues. Even this new sociology paid insufficient attention, however, to the nature and processes of war and war-preparation themselves. The new sociology of war, drawing many of its materials from social history, has presented itself very often as a development from, and even a variant of, the historical sociology of the state. Certainly the theoretical impetus to the new interest in war has been the changing direction of thinking about the state.

It is a remarkable fact, of parallel and equally striking importance to the neglect of total war, that in the depths of the totalitarian epoch sociology had little to say about the nature of the modern state. Even more fundamentally, of course, the issues of power and power-holding groups were hardly confronted in mid-century sociology. These issues were only slowly recovered, notably in and following Mills's *The Power Elite*; but it was not until the late 1960s and even the 1970s that a serious debate developed about the state. Modern state theory then emerged primarily, but never exclusively, from the rebirth of Marxism. The 1970s debate was mainly between Marxists, 'instrumentalist', 'structuralist' and 'state-derivatist'. In this debate, the key issues were the relationships between capital, classes and state power, and more specifically the forms of these relationships in modern (that is, 'post-war') capitalism. War and militarism were never central concerns.[7]

The neglect of war and militarism in this case reflected both the theoretical origins of Marxism and the particular context of the new state theory. Marxism was itself a product of the long nineteenth-century peace: it shared the characteristic of much classical social theory that socio-economic issues predominated over political and military concerns. More particularly, Western Marxism had emerged from a socio-cultural 'detour' which, as Anderson argues, avoided core political problems.[8] The core problems with which it failed to grapple were those of the epoch of totalitarianism – and total war. Western Marxism finally flowered, moreover, in the one decade between 1940 and 1990 in which the actuality of fear of global war was not a dominant social theme. One should not underestimate the extent to which *détente*, as well as affluence, was a condition for the radicalism of the late 1960s and early 1970s, of which the Marxist revival was a product. The Vietnam War had the paradoxical effect of pushing the general issue of modern warfare, especially in its nuclear form, to one side.

Marxist critics have themselves pointed out the inadequacy of the new state theory, which neglected the 'national', 'external' and 'inter-state' dimensions of state power.[9] As, in the later 1970s and the 1980s, social theory came to terms with these realities, the tendency was, however, to reject the terms of the Marxist debate. None of the major writers were hostile, politically or intellectually, to Marxism, and all wished to incorporate what are seen as the valid contributions of the Marxist discussion. But they did reject the assumption that Marxism provides a sufficient framework for state theory – or for a radical politics.

Two major reference points in this debate are undoubtedly Theda Skocpol's *States and Social Revolutions* and Michael Mann's *The Sources of Social Power*.[10] Skocpol reversed the Marxist formula of debate by explaining social revolutions in terms of crises of state power, themselves seen as contingent on international, war-related events. Her argument implied that the state had far more than the 'relative autonomy' from capital assumed by the Marxist debate. (She sufficiently impressed Ralph Miliband for him to propose a compromise between Marxism and the new state theory, in which capital and the state are seen as autonomous centres of power working in 'partnership' with each other.)[11] Skocpol's subsequent work stressed state-centredness, in that states must be seen as conglomerations of administrative and political power *sui generis*, irreducible to economic power; but the international/military context of state power became a more subordinate theme in the much-cited collaborative volume *Bringing the State Back In*.[12]

Mann, on the other hand, provided a sustained challenge to Marxist assumptions in arguments which give war and militarism a central place. For him, states were above all about military power, and there was only a contingent relationship between this and economic power. In a series of essays he challenged the view that there are necessary links between capitalism and militarism, or between domestic and international politics.[13] His arguments are constructed around a scheme of the phases of modern warfare, and so bring war back into the foreground of social theory.

Mann's theory of warfare and society, however schematic it remains at this point, makes him unusual among state theorists. The only comparable contribution to the social theory of war has come from a writer with a very different starting point. Mary Kaldor, the defence analyst and peace movement activist, argued for analysis of the 'mode of warfare' and its interaction with the mode of production. She argued, following Clausewitz's tantalizing remarks about the analogies between war and commerce, that we can see warfare as a social process comparable with the process of production. The central problem of war, especially modern war, is that opportunities for testing the values of weapons and strategies are far more limited and irregular than those for testing the values of commodities. This, Kaldor argued, causes particular difficulties in the nuclear age, leading to 'baroque' military technology and an imbalance between the modes of warfare and production which may be dangerous to peace.[14]

Kaldor's argument, although using Marxist-influenced terminology, was non-reductionist and non-Marxist in its basic theoretical assumptions. She could better be described as a radical Clausewitzian, so long as it is understood that the way in which she uses Clausewitz's understanding of war is very different from that of military strategists and classical Marxists alike. She presents some of the elements of a war-centred, rather than capital, or even state-centred, social theory, but very much in outline form. (I attempted to take this argument further in my own *Dialectics of War*.)[15]

## Giddens on war and the state

Anthony Giddens's work was a particularly important contribution to this debate on the social theory of war, both in general and in relation to the state. *The Nation-State and Violence* is by far the most complete statement, not just of Giddens's own thinking, but of these issues in relation to the main traditions of sociological thought as a whole.[16] Giddens places himself clearly alongside those, like Skocpol and Mann, who are attempting a non-economic reductionist theory of state power, and takes up the same general issues of the role of international relations and war in the analysis of states. He extends the challenge to Marxism which these writers have made, and invites the same incomprehension of Marxists such as Bob Jessop, who complains that he 'curiously neglects the modern welfare state in favour of the modern warfare state'.[17]

Giddens's work is distinguished, above all, because it locates these issues within a synthetic sociological theory and a generalized critique of previous positions which marginalized war and militarism (chiefly but not only Marxism). Giddens is concerned, however, with power and states, rather than with a theory of war as such. It is important to evaluate his work in this context, both to establish what he has achieved, and to identify the issues which his approach has not fully addressed.

It is interesting that Giddens's early work, while always identifying the state as a major problem of social theory, contained few indications of the centrality of the international and military context of state power. In *The Class Structure of Advanced Societies*, for example, Giddens contrasted Marx and Weber in terms of their treatments of state and society:

> The Marxian conception . . . treats the state essentially as an 'expression' of the class relationships generated in the market . . . whereas Marx viewed the state in terms of his pre-suppositions about the infrastructure of society, Weber tended to view that infrastructure in terms of a paradigm derived from his analysis of the state. For Weber the 'class principle' is subordinate to the 'bureaucratic principle'.[18]

But the Weberian model, to which Giddens inclines, does not appear at this stage to be connected to any particular concern with the state system in which states operate. In Giddens's short study of *Politics and Sociology in the Thought of Max Weber*, written in the same year, the only reference to war is a passing one:

> In the effects of the First World War upon German society, Weber saw both a vindication of his earlier analysis of the German social structure and the possibility of transforming the political order . . . . He made no secret of the positive sentiments which the 'great and wonderful' war inspired in him: the passivity, and the lack of a national political sense,

which he had criticised in the past, were replaced by a collective assertion of the integrity of the nation in the face of the other world powers.[19]

One will not find the terms 'war', 'militarism' or even 'violence' in the index to any of Giddens's work of the 1970s.

War and militarism appear to have become of interest to Giddens as he began to develop his own theory of power and to frame the terms of his critique of Marxism. In *A Contemporary Critique of Historical Materialism* he brings together a number of concerns in his work to focus on the nature of power and the state. He argues that power is routinely involved in the 'instantiation' of social practices: it is not a secondary characteristic of social life. Giddens also insists that 'power was never satisfactorily theorised by Marx, and that this failure is at the origin of some of the chief limitations of his scheme of historical analysis.'[20]

In this volume, Giddens introduces some of the principal axes of his later approach to the state. Modifying Foucault's view of power, he argues that 'surveillance', the capacity for 'storage of authoritative resources', is a key attribute of modern states. 'Lack of analysis of the phenomenon of surveillance ... is one of the major limitations of Marx's interpretation of the state.'[21] Surveillance is not just a feature of late, computerized, capitalist society, but integral to the history of capitalism.[22] He quotes Foucault: 'the traditional, ritual, costly, violent forms of power ... were superseded by a subtle, calculated technology of subjection.'[23]

The concept of surveillance is linked by Giddens, however, to a number of other theoretical propositions. On the one hand, it is argued, in terms quite compatible with Marx, that 'the insulation of economy from polity involves ... the extrusion of the means of violence from the principal axis of class exploitation, the capital/wage-labour relation.'[24] On the other, Giddens attacks 'the prevalence in nineteenth-century social thought of the notion that capitalistic economic enterprise is essentially non-violent in nature.' This apparent paradox is explained by the fact that 'Such a view ignores the

processes that led to the internal pacification of states . . . .
And it ignores the fact that the capitalist state has been the
purveyor of violence externally . . . .'[25]

The opposition of 'surveillance' and 'violence' thus assumes
a signal importance in Giddens's thought. The growth of state
surveillance corresponds to the reduction of violence within
societies ('pacification') and in particular within class relations.
But – and this is perhaps the most radical element of Giddens's
argument – the pacification of societies by states does not
imply a general pacification of social life. The reason for this,
once the violence of the initial pacification process itself has
subsided, is the *external* violence of the state. Here, given the
theoretical importance accorded to violence in society, is to be
found the source of the growing theoretical importance of war
to Giddens. When he remarks, later, that

> I have long contended that the neglect of what any casual
> survey of history shows to be an overwhelmingly obvious
> and chronic trait of human affairs – recourse to violence and
> war – is one of the most extraordinary blank spots in social
> theory in the twentieth century,[26]

Giddens is not simply making a ritual comment on a lack in
social theory. He is pointing to a factor which, his theory
suggests, is directly related to the main trends of contemporary
society.

The changing balance of internal and external violence, and
the changing role of the state, implies a major change in
the character of military power. 'In class-divided societies',
Giddens suggests, 'open class struggle is generally very sporadic,
though it may be very violent.'[27] Because of this violence, and
the lack of developed surveillance,

> Military power has normally placed a decisive role in the
> integration of class divided societies . . . . The use or the
> threat of the use of violence in sustaining system integration
> is ever present in class-divided societies. This is of major
> importance to the conceptualisation of the state . . . .[28]

In capitalism, by contrast, class struggles are a chronic feature
of the organization of production, but they are correspondingly
less violent, and they are regulated mainly by surveillance
rather than by violence. Military power no longer plays a
decisive role in system integration. The growth of military
power continues, however, and can only be explained by
external conflict.

It is clear that Giddens differs sharply from Marxists who
have tended to present the growth of military power as a result
of the sharpening of class contradictions, often neglecting in
the process the more obvious war-related explanations for the
growth of military power. If he considers the role of military
power within capitalist societies, he is more likely to see it as
cause than consequence. For example, he makes the point that
military organization anticipated the organization of the
factory:

> In the army barracks, and in the mass coordination of men
> on the battlefield (epitomised by the military innovations of
> Prince Maurice of Orange and Nassau in the sixteenth
> century) are to be found the prototype of the regimentation
> of the factory – as both Marx and Weber noted.[29]

Giddens also now presents the state specifically as a 'nation-
state'. He sees 'the period of triumph of capitalism as a "world
capitalist economy" as 'also a period eventuating in the worldwide triumph of the nation-state as a focus of political and
military organisation.'[30] And he argues that it is 'not necessary
(nor is it legitimate) to suppose that one has to unearth how it
came to be that capitalism "needed" the nation-state for
its development, or in which, *per contra*, the nation-state
"needed" capitalism.'[31] Nor is nationalism the direct product
of nation-states (still less of capitalism): this too needs to be
specifically explained, perhaps as a result of war. War
mobilization disrupts the social fabric – 'the relatively fragile
fabric of ontological security may become broken. In such
conditions regressive forms of object-identification [nationalism]
tend to come to the fore.'[32]

In this volume, therefore, Giddens outlines many of the positions on state and society which mark him off not just from Marx but also from others who acknowledge Weber as the major figure in social theory. What Giddens takes from Weber is quite clearly a world away from Parsons's interpretation, for example:

> Neither Weber's sombre view of modern capitalism, nor his emphases upon the centrality of military power and violence more generally in history, survive prominently either in Parsons's representations of Weber's work, or in Parsons's own theories.[33]

The centrality of war, military power and violence had not been so apparent in Giddens's earlier work, either, but now these are becoming the cutting edges of his theory of state and society.[34]

## 'The Nation-State and Violence'

Not surprisingly, the second volume of the 'contemporary critique of historical materialism' bears directly on these themes and contains a full exposition of Giddens's views. The more radical theoretical developments were, arguably, made in the first volume, but *The Nation-State and Violence* integrates them in a broad theoretical and historical statement. The gap between his theory and Marxism is also clarified.

At the centre of Giddens's theory, now, is the nation-state, presented not just as a major institution or set of institutions, but as *the* defining and integrating institution of modern societies. 'Modern societies', he writes, 'are nation-states, existing within a nation-state system.'[35] Societies were not previously co-extensive with administrative units, since traditional states lacked clearly defined boundaries and means of social control. It is a result of 'distinctive forms of social integration associated with the nation-state' that this has come about.[36]

'Capitalism' needs, in Giddens's view, to be 'prised free from the general framework of historical materialism, and integrated in a different approach to previous history and to the analysis of modern institutions.'[37] It becomes instead one of four ' "institutional clusterings" associated with modernity: heightened surveillance, capitalistic enterprise, industrial production and the centralised control of the means of violence'.[38] These clusterings are irreducible, the one to the other, but reflect different forces which are at work in modern societies. Two of these clusterings, of course, directly appertain to the nation-state (surveillance and military violence); the other two, which are more commonly used to define modern societies (industrialism and capitalism), 'intersect with' the development of the nation-state system.

States in general can be defined, following Weber rather than Marx, according to violence and territoriality, but Giddens wishes to qualify his definition. Traditional states, he argues, could 'claim' a legitimate monopoly of violence within a given territory, but only modern nation-states have really achieved it.[39] Traditional states were characterized by specialized military forces, but the distinction between external and internal war was not always very clear. The monopoly of violence eluded the central state, and much warfare was the result of attempts by states to establish and maintain as well as to extend the scope of their power. On the other hand, states did not 'govern' their populations in a regular sense, and so had periodically to resort to military force as a substitute for administration.

The fundamental transition, according to Giddens, is from the traditional state to the modern nation-state. The absolutist state is a stage in this development, but is still basically a traditional form. This transition is not determined by a single socio-economic process, or indeed by socio-economic processes in general. Giddens is determinedly non-reductionist in his explanation for changes in state forms, and one of the most interesting points in his account is where he argues that 'there were three sets of military developments that decisively influenced (but were also influenced by) the rise of the absolutist state.'[40] He refers to technological changes in armaments, the emergence of modern military discipline and the development of naval strength. He goes on to assert that

> Various main features of European state development were shaped in a decisive way by the contingent outcomes of military confrontations and wars. Nothing shows more clearly how implausible it is to regard the emergence of modern societies as the result of some sort of evolutionary scheme that inexorably led from the alluvial dirt of Sumer to the factory shop-floor of latter-day Europe.[41]

A crucial analytical issue in this assertion is whether military events should be regarded as purely 'contingent' or whether there is a major category of factors which need to be incorporated into the explanation of social change. Should military factors as such, or only the outcome of particular battles and wars, be regarded as 'contingent'? Giddens pursues his analysis of military developments, such as the development of standing armies and discipline, in a way which suggests that these are significant general factors. Repeating the historical point already made in *A Contemporary Critique* he writes that, through the interventions of Maurice of Nassau,

> there is a very real sense in which ... the techniques of Taylorism became well embedded in the sphere of the armed forces several hundred years before, in industrial production, they came to be known by that label.[42]

The development of modern nation-states, aided by military organization and technology, involves in Giddens's view the establishment of monopolies of violence. Nation-states as 'bordered power-containers' achieve more and more effective surveillance of their societies and are able to eliminate or marginalize violence within them. Civil wars in modern nation-states are, according to Giddens, less common than were the internal armed struggles of traditional states and societies. Where they do occur, the fact that armed movements are invariably concerned with the assumption of state power testifies to the centrality of the state in the modern world.

Giddens is 'principally concerned with the means of violence associated with the activities of organised armed forces, not with violence as a more blanket category of doing physical harm to others', and hence can discount (though he denies wishing to underplay) 'violence that takes place in smallscale contexts in modern societies'.[43] He mentions violent crime and domestic violence; it is obviously crucial to his theory that it should be possible also to discount class, industrial, political and racial violence.

The elimination of violence, or 'pacification' of societies by nation-states and their surveillance activities, are necessary conditions for the expansion of capitalism and industrialism. Indeed capitalism, according to Giddens, involves

> a novel type of class system, one in which class struggle is rife but also in which the dominant class . . . do not have or require direct access to the means of violence to sustain their rule. Unlike previous systems of class domination, production involves close and continuous relations between the major class groupings. This presumes a 'doubling-up' of surveillance, modes of surveillance becoming a key feature of economic organisations and of the state itself.[44]

Marx, of course, was aware of how the 'dull compulsion' of economic relations, rather than violence, was the main mechanism of capitalist power; but according to Giddens, The does not ask what happens to the means of violence "extruded" from the labour contract.'[45]

This 'admittedly crude formulation' echoes closely words used in *A Contemporary Critique*, already quoted, and expresses one of Giddens's most radical ideas. It is almost as thought he is suggesting that the violence which is squeezed out of society, and notably economic relations, is directly expressed in externally directed military violence, that is, in war. It is not, surely, that he believes that there is a fixed amount or level of violence in any society. What he is arguing is that the pacification of social relations occurs primarily through the accumulation of power in the nation-state. Although the mature form of a pacified society is one in which surveillance is paramount, the initial pacification occurs partly through military power, and leads to a standing army as the foundation of the modern nation-state. At the same time, Giddens argues that nation-states exist only in and through the nation-state system. He attacks Wallerstein's concept of a world-system, arguing that a world-system 'is not only formed by transnational economic connections and dependencies, but also by the global system of nation-states, neither of which can be exhaustively reduced to the other.'[46]

This argument gives Giddens a novel angle on an old debate. Mann, for example, has argued that, contrary to both the nineteenth-century 'optimistic theory of pacific capitalism' and the early twentieth-century Marxist theory of militaristic capitalism', industrial capitalism is intrinsically neither pacific nor militarist.[47] Giddens, by contrast, argues that industrial capitalism is 'pacific' – but only internally, within a nation-state:

> What it involves, however, is not the decline of war but a concentration of military power 'pointing outwards' towards other states in the nation-state system.[48]

Pacification and militarism are not alternatives, but two sides of the same process. This implies, however, that military power itself has undergone immense change.

Giddens devotes a chapter to the historical sociology of military power, outlining the development of armaments and military technology. Locating these within his four 'institutional clusters', he rejects the common assumption that capitalism lies behind the growth of arms, insisting instead that 'industrial capitalism provided the means for the industrialisation of war, but the activities and involvements of nation-states are at the origin of the phenomenon.'[49] He also emphasizes the link between military duty and citizenship rights in political democracy. In discussing the two World Wars, he stresses the

impact of war on industrial organization, the institutionalization of class conflict and the political structures of the
combatant states. 'My main point', he argues, 'is to emphasise
that the impact of war in the twentieth century upon
generalised patterns of change has been so profound that it is
little short of absurd to interpret such patterns without
systematic reference to it.'[50]

It is obviously of critical importance to discover how far this
impact continues beyond the period of the two World Wars.
'Do we', Giddens asks, 'still, in fact, live in military societies?'
'How far are Western nation-states currently dominated by
military imperatives in terms of their basic economic organisation? Are patterns of military rule likely to become more,
rather than less common . . . ?'[51]

In answering these questions, Giddens deals mainly with the
economic issue, arguing that, despite the specific weight of
military industries, economies as wholes are not generally
dominated by a 'military-industrial complex'; and, with the
political aspect, maintaining that even where the military take
power, rule is not generally carried out through military
means. Consistent with his main argument, he asserts that
military power as such is of declining importance in social
control. Repressive military regimes are examples of the more
general phenomenon of totalitarianism, which is inherent in
the surveillance state. Giddens concludes that only in the sense
that our nation-states are part of a world military order, in
which the means of waging industrialized war are widely
diffused, do we live today in 'military societies'. (In terms of
the internal organization of national societies, we are moving
in a 'post-military' direction, although he does not use this
term.)[52]

The system of nation-states – rather than capitalism or
industrialism – is, then, the key to understanding the problems
of military power. The role of the military in the newer 'state-
nations' depends on the same twin features of centralized,
bureaucratized military power and a historically high level of
internal pacification which are found in nation-states generally.
Despite the extent to which some states are militarily and

politically subordinate to others, and despite elements of international organization, world society is more than ever composed of competing nation-states with the means to wage industrialized war.

This analysis leads Giddens to largely pessimistic conclusions. 'In terms of historical agencies of change', he writes, 'there is no parallel in the sphere of weaponry to the proletarian in the area of industrial labour. No plausible "dialectical counterpart" to the progressive accumulation of military power seems to exist.'[53] Peace movements are likely, in Giddens's view, to be of limited effect. Hope is sought, however, in resistance to militaristic values – old-style militarism is seen as in decline, new-style militarism as no more than a propensity to seek or accept military solutions. In the absence of a dialectic of change, we must look to 'a renewal of utopianism, mixed with the firmest form of realism' to resist the war-propensities of nation-states.[54] This utopianism 'can (not *must*) negatively affect tactical decisions relevant to coping with a heavily militarised world.'[55]

## Dialectics of total war

It will be evident that *The Nation-State and Violence* has a very wide scope and offers an impressive range of generalizations – matched, it should be stated, by the breadth of its author's historical knowledge. In its restoration of the issues of war and militarism to the centre of social theory in general, and state theory in particular, it is far and away the most important text yet published. Its basic theoretical approach has been questioned, however, by Jessop, who argues that

> we seem to be faced with the concept of a gradual co-evolution of four different spheres without any serious attempt to move beyond an historical account to an analysis of system integration around the *capitalist* character of modern societies.[56]

There seem to be two separate issues here. One is whether

Giddens has adequately identified, and explained the relationships of, his 'institutional clusterings'. It is possible to argue, as this chapter does in relation to war and militarism, with the way the four are specified and to suggest better explanations for their interactions. But Jessop clearly wants to go further than this. As a Marxist, forced to admit that Giddens has made 'compelling' criticisms of historical materialism, he feels obliged to insist that it is around the 'capitalist' character of modern societies that system integration must be identified.

Giddens, however, has given compelling reasons for structuring our explanations of social integration – and social change – around the nation-state rather than around capitalism. It is not an oversight that prevented him from arguing as Jessop suggests. As our preliminary discussion has indicated, his argument brings together main points which are increasingly common ground among state theorists. *The Nation-State and Violence* is a persuasive statement of the new theoretical consensus based on the widely perceived inadequacies of Marxist state theory.

It is perhaps surprising that Jessop hinged his criticism on the relation between capitalism and the state, rather than examining the more novel parts of Giddens's argument such as his use of violence, war and militarism. A great deal, after all, rests on the dispute concerning pacification and surveillance. Giddens is adopting very broad historical standards when he dismisses class, industrial, political, racial, criminal or personal violence in contemporary societies as not amounting to significant violence for his purposes. When he accepts the Marxist concept of class struggle, but denies there is significant class violence, he identifies violence narrowly with organized, armed fighting and killing.

The distinction between what is commonly described in contemporary societies as 'social violence', and violence in this more fundamental sense is valid and important. But it is still unclear that Giddens is on strong historical ground. It would have been difficult for him to put forward his argument at an earlier stage in the development of nation-states and capitalism. In the first half of the twentieth century, organized class violence – for example, between the paramilitary formations of communist and Fascist parties – was all too commonplace. Class struggle appeared as likely to culminate in political violence as it did in pacification and integration. It is not so clear, then, that these are features of nation-states as such, rather than of the more industrially advanced nation-states since the Second World War. May not pacification also be regarded as a contingent military outcome?

What these issues demonstrate is that, while *The Nation-State and Violence* presents itself as a synthesis, it is often raising fundamental historical and analytical issues rather than resolving them. If this is true of its observations on social violence, it is even more true of the analysis of war and militarism. These themes are in reality far more problematic than Giddens allows. For him, they are a means of explaining important features of the modern nation-state, but they are still not treated coherently from a theoretical point of view. Because of the new importance accorded to military power as one of the core institutional clusterings of modern societies, it is necessary to develop a social theory of war and militarism.

Despite many assertions of the striking effects of war on society, Giddens never enters into the theory of war: to seek, for example, the sociological meaning of Clausewitz, whose concept of war could be set alongside the ideas of Marx and Weber as an intellectual landmark for the modern era. He therefore lacks a general explanation for the facts which in so many ways he finds of startling importance for understanding modern societies.

There is a broad similarity between Giddens's concept of military power as an institutional cluster and Kaldor's of a 'mode of warfare'. The difference is that, where Giddens offers us a series of historical accounts of military technology, organization, etc., Kaldor argues for seeing warfare as a set of social processes flowing from the contest of violence between states. Giddens writes of the concentration of outward-pointing military violence in the state, but he does not discuss the logic of its use in actual war. This is where, as Kaldor recognizes, Clausewitz is essential.[57]

Clausewitz's main contribution is not to be sought, as Marxists have believed, in his dictum that 'war is the continuation of policy by other means'. The core of his work is his concept of warfare as a contest of force, to which there is no necessary limit. War may be limited, by the political aims of the combatants and also by what Clausewitz calls 'friction', that is, constraints such as geography, climate, logistics and technology. But the essence of war is the contest of force which *tends* to become absolutely destructive. 'Absolute war' is not therefore merely one type of war, but the logical culmination of the inner meaning of war. 'Absolute war' can therefore be seen as an 'ideal type' or a 'maximum possible concept' of war in general. Clausewitz may not have envisaged that absolute war would ever be fully realized in practice: but, as Howard points out, nuclear war threatens to abolish friction and make war instantaneously absolute.[58]

The absolutism of war is a fact of general sociological interest. It is this which accounts for the tendency of war to cut through established patterns of social relations. The logic of violence dwarfs other social concerns, so that both formal and informal social institutions undergo change in response to the demands of warfare. Wars are often major periods of social change: this has long been true, but the nature of modern warfare and its relationship to society have given the point new significance. Twentieth-century industrialized war raises the stakes in the military determination of social relations. Giddens recognizes the manifestations of this process, but his theory does not fully explain it.

The concept of the mode of warfare is extremely important here. Kaldor lays emphasis on the way in which the form of war being waged or envisaged in strategic planning becomes embedded in military technology and stresses the way in which it reflects historically outmoded strategic concerns, thus rendering itself militarily obsolescent and economically retarding.[59]

What is needed is a more general account of the 'mode of warfare' which developed as a result of the rise of the nation-state system and of industrial capitalism, and of the way this has changed over time. I have suggested that we need to develop the sociological concept of *total war* to describe this mode of warfare, incorporating both Clausewitzian and socio-historical insights.[60] On the one hand, the development of military technology, under the impact of the industrialization of war, led to warfare which increasingly realized the ideal type of 'absolute war'. On the other hand, capitalist organization of an industrial workforce, combined with the mobilizing power of the nation-state (a form of what Giddens calls surveillance), created the potential not just for mass armies but for total socio-economic and political war mobilization.

These two dimensions combine to define the mode of total war which dominated the economic, social and political life of the first half of the twentieth century and which was realized in the two World Wars. Total war was not of course a single form of war, but was constantly changing. Between the two World Wars, developments in strategy and technology changed national labour forces from the suppliers of total war to its targets. Revolutionary ideologies, by-products of the First World War, became motive forces of the Second. These and other changes marked inner transformations of total war and its relationship to society.

Much of Giddens's analysis could be further explicated by a dynamic concept of total war, attempting to relate the international, military, political-ideological and socio-economic processes involved. Total war was, moreover, a deeply contra-dictory process, leading to both revolutionary and reformist social movements. Giddens is wrong to deny the significance of revolutionary violence in capitalist societies in the first part of the twentieth century. A more satisfactory argument against Marxism is that revolutionary contradictions were much more apparent in mobilization for total war than in the capitalist economic crisis which Marxists have seen as determining. Total war was also, however, the context for much of the consolidation of the power of nation-states of which Giddens writes. Indeed, and this again is a question-mark against Marxism, the outcome of class, as much as military, violence in the epoch of total war has invariably been to centralize state power.

The criticism of Giddens is that, while he recognizes many of the effects of total war, he does not explain what total war is or has been. The nature of military power, as a basic institutional cluster of modern society, is explained only *ad hoc* and not theoretically (on a par with capitalism, industrialism or even surveillance). Military power tends to be presented as a resource of states; it is not clear that Giddens has quite come to terms, theoretically at least, with the destructive logic of actual war. He has not thought through an answer to the question why and how is it that modern war has such a transformative effect on social relations?

Just as Giddens lacks a clear concept of the mode of warfare and its development historically, he only skirts around the changes which have taken place since 1945. He grasps, with his seemingly unerring sense for the historical tendency, the demise of classical militarism which accompanied the passing of classical total war. He puts his finger on the paradox of societies which, while producing an ever more destructive outward-pointing militarism, are not inwardly militarist in most obvious senses – indeed are quite clearly post-militarist. He does not, however, discuss either the causes of this in the nuclear mutation of total warfare, or the consequences for nation-states. In this respect Giddens has less to offer than Mann, who has recently outlined a scheme of the stages of modern warfare.[61] (Mann's threefold classification – 'Clausewitzian', 'citizen' and 'nuclear' war – is, however, open to question both on interpretation and argument.)[62]

What cannot be in doubt is that the period since the end of the Second World War has seen a fundamental transition, in the advanced industrial societies, from mass-mobilization to high-technology militarism. Nuclear weaponry was the first, and is still the dominant, but is by no means the only technology of this new form of war-preparation. Warfare has in general moved beyond the stage in which quantities of men and weapons are crucial to the supremacy of technological sophistication – in electronics as well as nuclear physics.

The transformation of modern warfare clearly has major implications for the relationship of war and society. Nuclear militarism clearly requires general ideological mobilization, in the context of Cold War rivalry, and this can give the impression of societies which are still highly militarized. At the same time there is a need for specialized military industries of a high order of technological sophistication, which lie behind the concept of a 'military-industrial complex'. Indeed, these two characteristics, taken together, led E. P. Thompson to assert that societies in the Cold War 'do not have military-industrial complexes; they are military-industrial complexes.'[63]

This view, understandable in view of the danger which war-preparation poses, is, however, misleading. Ideological mobilization accompanies practical demobilization: populations are no longer mobilized *en masse* in war-preparation, nor will they be required to fight and produce in nuclear war. The concentration of military industry in high technology means that it has less direct impact on advanced economies as wholes. In order to prepare for possible wars, nation-states no longer require much of the direct and detailed control over economies and societies which they took in the epoch of classical total war.

Giddens clearly appreciates some of this change, but his analysis cannot pinpoint the issues decisively enough. The difficulty is that his concepts are at too high a level of generality to explain specific phases and forms of the relationships of nation-state and society. The relationships of military power, surveillance, industrialism and capitalism are changing in ways which are descriptively acknowledged, but cannot be accounted for theoretically. For example, Giddens is right to argue that modern nation-states rule through surveillance rather than military power. But surveillance takes many forms: the fact that nuclear nation-states such as the USA and the UK can dispense with much of the direct control which they assumed forty years ago is of immense political importance. More sophisticated forms of surveillance, monitoring and manipulation – without post-war 'intervention' and controls – have opened up a new economic and political era in advanced Western nation-states. The ideology of Thatcherism, with its twin totems of nuclear weapons and the market, actually expressed the new relationship of the nuclear state to economy and society. The state may retain overall direction of the national economy while abdicating much of its detailed intervention to private agencies. Giddens offers us little with which to define these changes, or their relationship to military power.

One point on which Giddens is clear is his denial that there are dialectics of change in military power and war. It has been argued here, against this, that there certainly have been radical contradictions in the mode of warfare. Total war (very ironically from the point of view of Marxism) was the context of socialist advance in the first half of this century. It is common ground, however, that contemporary nuclear militarism will not generate any internal agency for change: the radical contradictions of war mobilization have been closed off. It is not so clear, however, that the changed relation of war and society is so hopeless for radical politics. The decline of classical militarism, and the development of post-military society, also creates space in which a politics of transformation can flourish.

Similarly, although the retreat of the nuclear state from much direct socio-economic control is designed to create new opportunities for private capitalism, it also brings into being new space for a decentralizing politics of democratic control. It may make it possible, for almost the first time in this century, to define socialism free from the distortions of statism induced by total war. This may be, as Giddens insists, largely a utopian exercise, but the link with historical possibility is still there to be shaped.

From a theoretical point of view, the central issue which is raised by these critical reflections is that of how far *The Nation-State and Violence*, in correcting the neglect of war and the inter-state dimension of state-power, overemphasized the predominance of the nation-state system and minimized its social contradictions. A world of nation-states, each internally pacified (by extensive surveillance) but potentially engaged in the most violent war with one another, is a world in which states are all and social forces are nothing. No wonder that the theory has been seen as a sociological underpinning for a realist view of global anarchy. In centring on the global system of nation-states, the approach leaves little room for a wider concept of global *society*.

*The Nation-State and Violence* is perhaps best seen, then, as a theoretical summing-up of the global state system as it emerged from the period of total war. It presents us with a schema of state and society which enables us to understand the 'national societies' into which the world was divided in the era of total war, and which still predominated in the Cold War period.[64] Like all such schema, it was a good starting point for analysis, but it had its weaknesses. These were not so serious so long as the major conditions underpinning it remained intact, but are more critical now that fundamental changes have started to occur since the end of the Cold War. As we now look at the very different world of the 1990s and beyond, we need to re-evaluate the theory of the state bequeathed to us from the 1980s.

# NOTES

1   Fred Halliday, 'State and society in international relations: a second agenda', *Millenium* 16, 2, 1987, pp. 215–29; Andrew Linklater, *Beyond Realism and Marxism*, London: Macmillan, 1990. See also Michael Banks and Martin Shaw, eds, *State and Society in International Relations*, Hemel Hempstead: Harvester-Wheatsheaf, 1991.

2   Faruk Yalvaç, 'The sociology of the state and the sociology of international relations'. In Banks and Shaw, eds, *State and Society in International Relations*, p. 94.

3   Anthony Giddens, *The Nation-State and Violence*, Cambridge: Polity, 1985.

4   See Arthur Marwick, *War and Social Change in the Twentieth Century*, London: Macmillan, 1977, and *Britain in the Century of Total War*, London: Bodley Head, 1968.

5   Michael Mann argues that modern sociology has selected those

strands of nineteenth-century theory, liberal and Marxist, which make these assumptions, while neglecting others, which he calls militarist, which challenge them: 'War and social theory'. In Colin Creighton and Martin Shaw, eds, *The Sociology of War and Peace*, London: Macmillan, 1987, pp. 54–72.

6   See Shaw and Creighton, Introduction, ibid.

7   Martin Shaw, 'War, imperialism and the state system: a critique of orthodox Marxism for the 1980s'. In Shaw, ed., *War, State and Society*, London: Macmillan, 1984, pp. 47–70.

8   Perry Anderson, *Considerations on Western Marxism*, London: New Left Books, 1976.

9   Shaw, 'War, imperialism and the state system', pp. 47–70.

10  Theda Skocpol, *States and Social Revolutions: A Comparative Analysis of France, Russia and China*, Cambridge: Cambridge University Press, 1979; Michael Mann, *The Sources of Social Power*, Cambridge: Cambridge University Press 1985.

11  Ralph Miliband, *Class Power and State Power*, London: Verso, 1983, p. 70.

12  Peter B. Evans, Dietrich Rueschemeyer and Theda Skocpol, eds, *Bringing the State Back In*, Cambridge: Cambridge University Press, 1985.

13  Michael Mann, 'Capitalism and militarism'. In Shaw, ed., *War, State and Society*, pp. 25–46; 'War and Social Theory', op. cit.

14  Mary Kaldor, 'Warfare and capitalism'. In E. P. Thompson et al., *Exterminism and Cold War*, London: Verso, 1982; *The Baroque Arsenal*, London: Deutsch, 1982.

15  Martin Shaw, *Dialectics of War: An Essay on the Social Theory of War and Peace*, London: Pluto Press, 1988.

16  Anthony Giddens, *The Nation-State and Violence*, Cambridge: Polity, 1985 (hereafter *NSV*).

17  Bob Jessop, Review of *The Nation-State and Violence*, *Capital and Class*, 29, Summer 1986, pp. 216–17.

18  Giddens, *The Class Structure of Advanced Societies*, London: Hutchinson, 1974, pp. 124–5.

19  Giddens, *Politics and Sociology in the Thought of Max Weber*, London: Macmillan, 1972, p. 21.

20  Giddens, *A Contemporary Critique of Historical Materialism*, London: Macmillan, 1981.

21  Ibid., p. 5.

22  Ibid., p. 175.

23  Michel Foucault, *Discipline and Punish: The Birth of the Prison*, London: Allen Lane, 1977, pp. 220–1.

24  Giddens, *A Contemporary Critique of Historical Materialism*, p. 11.

25  Ibid., p. 12.

26  Ibid., p. 177.

27  Ibid., p. 130.

28  Ibid., pp. 163–4.

29  Ibid., p. 125.

30  Ibid., p. 182.

31  Ibid., p. 183.

32  Ibid., p. 194.

33  Ibid., p. 206.

34  Curiously, however, the indexing of these terms remains incomplete: only violence is – rather briefly – annotated in *A Contemporary Critique*, while 'war' and 'military' are unlisted. Even in *The Nation-State and Violence* there is no entry under 'military', while that under 'war' simply refers to other headings.

35  NSV, p. 1.

36  Ibid., p. 2.

37  Ibid., p. 1.

38  Ibid., p. 5.

39  Ibid., pp. 19, 27.

40  Ibid., p. 105.

41  Ibid., p. 112.

42  Ibid., p. 113.

43  Ibid., p. 121.

44  Ibid., pp. 159–60.

45  Ibid., p. 160.

46  Ibid., p. 169.

47  Mann, 'Capitalism and militarism', pp. 44–5.

48  *NSV*, p. 192.

49  Ibid., p. 226.

50  Ibid., p. 244.

51  Ibid., pp. 245–6.

52  See, however, Martin Shaw, *Post-Military Society*, Cambridge: Polity, 1991.

53  Ibid., p. 326.

54  Ibid., p. 334.

55  Ibid., p. 339.

56  Jessop, p. 219. Italics in the original.

57   Kaldor, 'Warfare and capitalism'.
58   Michael Howard, *Clausewitz*, Oxford: Oxford University Press, 1982.
59   Kaldor, *The Baroque Arsenal*.
60   Shaw, *Dialectics of War*.
61   Mann, 'The roots and contradictions of modern militarism', *New Left Review*, 162, March–April 1987, 35–50.
62   Shaw, *Dialectics of War*, ch. 4.
63   E. P. Thompson, 'Exterminism: the last stage of civilization'. In Thompson et al., *Exterminism and Cold War*.
64   The term Cold War is used here to describe the system of East–West conflict as it existed until 1989, and not just the periods of heightened tension as in the original Cold War of the late 1940s and early 1950s, or the Second Cold War of the 1980s.

*Three*

# State Theory and the Post-Cold War World

The international order of the twenty-first century will be radically different from that which we knew between 1945 and 1990. In place of the bipolar world, a new regime of states and international institutions is being forged – and with it new relationships of state and society. The outline of this world is only partially visible in the upheavals of the mid-1990s. The Soviet Union, the second superpower, which until recently constituted one pole of the old 'post-war' order, has disintegrated before the eyes of its former adversaries: after several years of upheaval, we do not yet know in what form the state system will be consolidated in its territories. The Cold War division of Europe has gone: Eastern Europe undergoes economic, political and even military fragmentation, while the West unites, however problematically, in the European Community. The United States, triumphant as the sole superpower, is nevertheless struggling to maintain its supremacy over its European and Japanese allies.

The role of war in this new world order is highly problematic. On the one hand, however strong the rivalries of the major Western powers are or may become, no one seriously believes that – even in the longer term – they will lead to war. Even realists and Marxists, an unholy theoretical alliance with a common interest in denying this assertion, can manage little more than caveats to it. The Western community of interest in a pacified world is being reinforced by institutionalization, economic and political as well as military. This generalization can be upheld, even if Western leaders stop woefully short of a positive assertion of its potential and seem, in many crises, actively to avoid concerted action.

Similarly, the collapse of the Soviet Union is a historic failure for the successor states, so that, however much they may find conflict among and within themselves, it is highly unlikely that – even with nuclear weapons – Russia, Ukraine, Kazakhstan and the others will pose a direct threat to Western interests. Like many other states – China, India, and the other major states of Asia, the major Latin American powers, even most of those in the Middle East – they are likely to look for an accommodation with and a role within the Western-dominated world economy and state system. For all these reasons, the era of big wars between core states in the world system seems over. The total war system of global state–society relationships, which survived in markedly attenuated form during the Cold War and the nuclearization of military technology, is finally passing. In its place, the core states of the West, and to a considerable degree many other parts of the world, are moving into a post-military relationship of state and society.[1]

On the other hand, however, it has rapidly become apparent that some regional and, even more, civil conflicts now have greater potential for war.[2] The removal of Cold War bloc discipline and the undermining of Cold War ideologies, especially communism, have thrown both the state system and state–society relations into new flux. The nation-state has been transformed from a relatively stable nexus of state–society relationships into the focus of the manifold instabilities of both the state system and civil society. In this new situation, the existing forms of state theory in both international relations and sociology are brought very decisively into question.

## The challenge to international relations theory

This new situation poses a major challenge to the ways in which we have learnt to understand the international order. The theory with which academic social scientists attempt to grasp these realities has been developed in the 'post-war' era. International relations has emerged as a discipline in the shadow of the Cold War. Even when it has not (as has sometimes been the case) taken on the propagandist tones of one side, it has inevitably been constrained by what have appeared the enduring realities of bipolar conflict. Even when writers attempted to see beyond the Cold War, they hardly imagined that it would collapse as suddenly as it did in the late 1980s, and few attempted until very recently to predict the shape of the post-Cold War world. In short, it is as if a charge has been placed under the categories of international relations theory: in the 1990s we can see the explosion, but we are not sure what will be left, and how useful it will be, when the dust settles.

Before major upheavals, the best theory is often that which, while it does not generate precise predictions of change, nevertheless sensitizes us to its dimensions. In the last years of the Cold War a ferment had begun in international relations, and much of this centred around the concept of the state. International relations theory had always known – or so it thought – what states were. Liberals knew that states existed to protect individuals from one another; realists that states protected themselves from one another. Identification of security with the state was almost complete, and the classical writers (and many others) had hardly felt the need to separate out categories such as 'society' or even 'nation' from that of 'state'. Because people thought they knew what 'state' meant, remarkably little attention was paid to exploring the concept and its ramifications.

In the 1980s, however, as the 'new' Cold War intensified, critical thinking about international relations also expanded. From a variety of different directions, writers began to problematize the state which, for realism especially, had been so taken for granted. Marxists had been largely responsible for a revival of critical theorizing about the state in the previous decade: not surprisingly, then, some attempts at new perspectives in international relations came from this point of view. Marxism appeared to represent a superior notion of the state, which was manifestly more serious in its attempt to integrate social assumptions than most traditional international relations views.

There were, however, three major difficulties with this approach. First, Marx and Engels, whose writings on the state in general were limited and fragmentary, produced virtually nothing on the international aspects of state. Second, Marxist theorists of the state – Leninists and Gramscians, instrumentalists and structuralists alike – however divided they were in other respects, were united in viewing it from within national societies, from the perspective of class. And third, Marxist views of the international were for the most part incorrigibly economist, defining the 'world-system' in terms of the global economy, and leaving little room for the system of states.[3] Some of the earliest attempts to bring Marxism into international relations, such as the work of Kubalkova and Cruickshank,[4] focused heavily on the official Marxist-Leninist doctrines of the Soviet Union and other communist states – now completely abandoned except for a few curious anachronisms, and of little use in any case to the kind of critical Marxism which Western theorists sought to develop.

A recent writer who looks for such a 'critical theory' argues that we need to go 'beyond realism *and* Marxism'.[5] Sharing the impulse for a view of the state which transcends traditional international relations categories, but generally critical of the Marxist conception of the state (especially as applied to international relations), a growing number of specialists have looked to reconstruct the theory of the state.[6] As Halliday demonstrates, the relationships between international relations and sociological theory are proving of critical importance to the reconstruction of state theory.[7] The emergence of a non-Marxist sociology of the state, represented by major works such as those of Skocpol, Giddens and Mann, has offered an alternative pole to both realism and Marxism.

These new directions were begun before the end of the Cold War. Although the theorizing is at a general level, the crisis and change of direction in the world-system provides a particularly sharp test of its relevance. How far do the new approaches help to explain the change itself and to understand the lines of the emerging new international order? Moreover, the most abstract theory responds, however indirectly, to historical circumstances, and it is to be expected that works written in the early 1980s (at the height of the 'Second Cold War') will reflect the very difficult conditions in which they were produced. How far are the limitations those of tone and emphasis, which are unavoidable, and how far are they real structural weaknesses?

## Sociology of the state and international relations

A major reason that the new sociology of the state is being taken seriously in international relations is that it, in turn, takes international relations — in the old-fashioned sense of relations between states — very seriously. Skocpol used the international relations between states, especially in war, to explain the internal breakdown of states in revolutions.[8] Mann explained that he preferred a geopolitical explanation of wars to either the 'optimistic theory of pacific capitalism' or the 'pessimistic theory of militaristic capitalism' emanating from sociology and Marxism respectively.[9] Giddens reinstated warfare as a basic 'institutional cluster' of modern societies, seeing it as a side of the nation-state which had been strengthened.[10]

In Mann's work, there is a polemical assertion of the autonomy of states as actors and of geopolitics as a basis of international relations, which, coupled with a denial of social-systemic factors, leads a sociological analysis towards realist conclusions. As Yalvaç points out, the convergence with traditional international relations views of the state, just when international relations theorists are moving away from them, may not necessarily be helpful; we do not have to accept his own preferred Marxist alternative to recognize the problem as real.[11]

With Giddens, who is less polemical about it, there is also a sense in which the analysis leads towards a world of warring nation-states, in which the autonomy of states from non-state actors has been increased. In his work, which has been most influential in international relations, the end-point also seems close to realism: violence is the arbiter of a world of nation-states. One might think that sociology had no more to offer to international relations than a more weighty, secure intellectual underpinning for positions which are under challenge within the discipline; paradoxically, the radical infusion of social categories may have effects which are intellectually conservative.

There is a real problem here, although the line of thought has (one hopes) only to be simplified in this way for its inadequacy to become apparent. The paradox can be unravelled to reveal a more progressive contribution. Firstly, we should recognize that the limitations of Mann's and Giddens's conclusions are the product of the direction in which they are travelling. Sociology has traditionally ignored (up to and including the Marxist debate on state theory) not merely international relations but the basic territorial aspect of the state. It has been necessary to insist on some truths which seem fairly elementary in international relations to get serious work going. The specific conclusions are less important than the direction of the argument.

Secondly, the theoretical infrastructure which has evolved can sustain a far wider range of developments than would be indicated by a simple realist reading. To see the state in its international aspect as related to definite social structuring changes the whole way in which we conceptualize the problems of international relations. And thirdly, the body of work in question signifies a breakthrough in the sociological understanding of international relations. Now this has occurred, it is possible to create a wider debate in which other, even quite contrasting, sociological contributions to international relations will be possible.

Thus once we see warfare as a basic social process and institutional context, it becomes possible to ask more specific questions about the relations of war, state and society than Giddens himself addresses. We can identify specific forms of warfare, such as total war (which is discussed in Chapter 2), through which their interaction is developed. When we look at such specific forms, the global trends towards 'surveillance' and 'warfare' seem more problematic. War is not just an outcome of trends towards the concentration of administrative and military power. War, in turn, acts on society, not just to mobilize it behind the state, but to accentuate social contradictions which in turn can threaten the state. The revolutionary tensions produced by war affect the nature of individual states and thus feed back in turn into international relations.

In this sense, a sociological account may offer more than a supporting argument for a view of inter-state relations: it may see the system of states as existing in complex interaction with society–state relations. The understanding of war is clearly a specific intellectual context of great significance in this debate. Traditionally, the discipline of international relations has seen it as the decisive means by which conflicts between states are resolved and major changes in the international system occur. The historical sociology of war sees it, in contrast, as an arena of social and political change, in which war mobilisation causes social upheaval which spills back into the state system.

The specific focus on war, as a context of both state and intrastate social action, may in fact lead us to revise Giddens's categories: 'surveillance' suggests a much too one-sided relationship between state and society. Although states have partially succeeded (but not as much as Giddens implies) in removing violent challenges, this 'pacification' does not mean passivity. Just as nation-states themselves have more active relationships to their societies – they mobilize as well as control and survey – so social groups act to modify states. This debate has, of course, developed within the framework of the Cold War world. It is probably not a coincidence, given their quasi-realist conclusions, that Giddens and Mann produced major works and much quoted articles in the early 1980s – when it would have been difficult not to have been impressed with the warlike potential of geopolitics. The argument about total war also bears the impress of its context, a world which had been so clearly shaped by the Second World War. As we have noted, the issue is whether the structure of the analyses also help us to address the new context into which international relations theory is now thrust.

There are two arenas in which we can examine this issue: the process of ending the Cold War itself, and the nature of the new international order which is now emerging. If the state theorists whom we have discussed, or sociological approaches in general, are relevant to international relations, then they must have important implications for these two key arenas.

## Social and international forces in the end of the Cold War

Intellectual battle has already been joined over the end of the Cold War. In some quarters, there have been celebrations for the victory of capitalism – and the 'end of ideology'. These apart, however, the theoretical issue is clearly raised: can we explain this great change in international relations in terms of international relations itself, or do we need a wider-based political science and sociology? As Cox points out, there is a superficial plausibility to the thesis that the USA under Reagan and Weinberger confronted the Soviet Union – and won. The tightening of the arms race, as a result of US rearmament, certainly increased the pressure on the ailing Soviet economy.[12] And yet to see the competitive inter-state level as self-sufficient and determining is to take a very narrow and ultimately unsatisfactory view of the breakthrough.

Clearly the end of the Cold War is above all the result of the implosion of the Soviet Union. This epoch-making crisis cannot be attributed – not even in its timing – solely or mainly to the pressure of the arms race. Indeed the arms race generated contradictory effects on the Soviet system: at the same time as it presented an increasingly intolerable economic pressure, it also provided much of the rationale for the regime. The discipline of Stalinism and Brezhnevism – in the subordination of eastern Europe as well as the basic political and ideological repression – was largely justified by the exigencies of military and political competition with its Western adversaries. The Cold War helped freeze the Soviet empire for four decades, even as it contributed some of the pressures towards its ultimate demise.

International competition in wider senses clearly played a larger part: but to draw attention to this raises problems for a classical international relations approach. The logic of the positions of the USSR and Eastern Europe in the world economy, and the example of freer intellectual, cultural and political life in the West, were both fundamental determinants of the change in the Soviet Union. Neither of these can be reduced to a 'state' effect: they were influences of global economic and cultural relations on the Soviet and Eastern European economies and cultures, to a considerable extent independent of the actions of Western states. Indeed one of the most fundamental reasons for the crisis of the Soviet system and the 'triumph' of the West was clearly the much greater impact of society on Western states, compared with the apparent insulation of Stalinist regimes from societal influences.

Equally important was the impact which societal influences on Western states had on international relations. This occurred in ways not always consistent with the triumphalist vision of Western ideologists. It can be seen most clearly in the contribution of peace movements in Western Europe in the early 1980s to a loosening of the North Atlantic alliance. These social movements, arising within Western states and in opposition to dominant policies, clearly influenced the whole climate of debate and policy-formation. Although in the short term (in 1981–3) the peace movements were clearly defeated in their immediate objective of preventing cruise missile deployment, in the longer term their ideology of pan-European peace and disarmament paved the way for the European dimension of Gorbachev's reform movement. Moreover the 'zero option' on intermediate nuclear weapons, proposed by Reagan to head off the peace movements, was picked up by Gorbachev and became, ironically, the basis for US–Soviet agreements. At the same time, the greater autonomy of Western European states within NATO encouraged the more European and reform-minded communists in the Soviet Union and Eastern Europe (for example in Hungary) to try to move their parties towards more independent positions beyond the Cold War.

The example of the peace movements in the West also played an important part in developments in the East. The Western movements helped stimulate small, more courageous unofficial peace and human rights groupings in Eastern Europe, many of whose activists were to play a part in the East German and Czechoslovak revolutions of 1989. The peace movements were a most important cutting edge of the re-emergence of civil society in communist states. This development, in turn, reflected deep social changes which had formed, throughout the Eastern bloc, educated intelligentsias excluded from power.

Complex societal and state pressures, working their way through to the international system, thus prepared the way for Gorbachev and the crisis of the Soviet system, and in turn for the end of the Cold War. There was therefore a critical interaction of what would conventionally be defined as 'social' and 'international' changes in the processes which led to the end of the Cold War. We can define this dialectic of civil society and the international system as, from a more developed theoretical perspective, the interrelationship of two major constellations within global society.

This interaction can also be seen in the actual events which led to the crumbling of the Berlin Wall in November 1989. The decisive initiatives which led to this event came, from 1985 onwards, from the top level of the Soviet state. It was also crucial that, once it became clear that Gorbachev really meant business, his disarmament proposals received an increasingly positive response from the United States and most Western European states. Equally importantly, his example in initiating reform within the Soviet state undermined the Stalinist system everywhere in Europe. It is difficult now to credit how Honecker and Jakes (the Stalinist leaders of East Germany and Czechoslovakia respectively), for example, imagined they could stand against this tide. That they did meant that Gorbachev had to play a direct part in signalling their departure, for example, during East Germany's ill-fated fortieth anniversary celebrations in October 1989.

Gorbachev, nevertheless, while he willed the fall of Honecker, hardly intended the instant reunification of Germany and the complete dissolution of communism in Europe. This draws our attention to the fact that, while states can control much of the process of change, they are ultimately subject to a much wider array of social forces. Gorbachev, from 1989 to 1991, seemed increasingly like the captain of a large and unwieldy old tanker, tossing in seas so turbulent that he could be washed overboard – his ship eventually breaking up and sinking. That no Gorbachev-type leader appeared in East Germany or Czechoslovakia meant that the people had to go on the streets, their unprecedentedly peaceful revolutions toppling the regimes and breaching the Wall. The totalitarian autonomy of Ceauşescu meant that reformers in Romania could take power only as a result of a bloody popular revolt. These interventions of the people were repeated in varying forms all over the Soviet Union, in the democratic and national movements of the Ukraine and Georgia as well as the Baltic states, and in Russia itself, in the events leading up to the unsuccessful coup of August 1991 and the end of communism.

The effects of these wider societal interventions in the state, internationally as well as domestically, are not all unequivocally benign. The internationalism of the end of the Cold War is matched by the resurgent nationalisms of half a continent. On the other hand, however, the positive effects on international relations of the East German and Czechoslovak revolutions are difficult to gainsay. Prepared by the dramatic changes at state level under Gorbachev, these social movements were nevertheless an essential and defining moment of the transition from the Cold War to the new international situation in which, as we have suggested, big wars between major powers are increasingly unthinkable.

## Social forces in post-Cold War international relations

As well as accounting for the process of change, a theory of the state needs to describe and explain the emerging new international situation itself. Of course, terms such as 'order' and 'system' imply a concept of stability and equilibrium. It is extremely doubtful that the new international situation can involve anything like the relative simplicity of the bipolar world at its most stable. For many years, analysts have described the changes in the international system in terms of growing fragmentation and complexity, with the gradual break-up of blocs and the emergence of additional regional powers (not to mention the proliferation of non-state actors). Now that the framework of blocs has been removed (almost), it is unrealistic to expect a new simplification. International relations may abhor a vacuum and seek a new hegemony, but this may be easier to call for than to define. One at least of the old superpowers is still alive and kicking, although the hegemony of the USA is still clearly in historic decline.

Expectations of a definitively new order have rested on the possibility of an overarching alliance of the USA, Europe (notably Germany) and Japan with the Soviet Union: a 'superbloc' of the industrial world which would dominate the divided regions of the 'developing world' and breathe new life into international institutions. The relatively united response, under clear US leadership, to the Gulf crisis in 1990–1 seemed a clear indication of this direction. The promise has been that (as within the European Union, where economic cooperation has helped inhibit old military rivalries) a 'security community' will be formed, among whose members the resort to war will become increasingly unthinkable, and the development of common military and political policies towards the rest of the world will become the norm.

It is likely that, despite conflicting economic interests which will make it extremely problematic and uneven at times, such a process may take place. Much of the old 'Third World' may acquiesce in it, in many situations, because of its close dependence on the great Western powers. But there are formidable regional rivalries which can issue in war, as the Middle East continues to demonstrate; and the continuing shifts of global population, productivity and military power which may be expected in the first half of the twenty-first century will make the mere 'containment' of the South, however powerful the bloc ranged against it, a very difficult business.

Only a much more radical restructuring of the international order than Western interests may contemplate, to allow for the development of the South and the representation of its interests in a genuinely global community, will ultimately guarantee a new and lasting stability. This process could be both threatened and assisted by internal transformation of nation-states. The democratization of China, for example, with its billion plus people, could be a tremendously positive process, but it could also pose problems for international order just as acute as the implosion of the Soviet Union. Indeed, one can go further and say that even the most positive changes in international relations and national political regimes can have acutely dangerous effects, as raised expectations generate rapid and often unforeseen socio-political responses.

The dark underside of the new instability, and the malignant potential of the interaction of emerging civil society with international change, can be seen quite clearly in many developments of the early 1990s. In the Caucasian republics of the former Soviet state, as well as in former Yugoslavia, the collapse of communism has led to new nationalist wars. In a crisis which is more than just the break-up of an empire, or even of a political and ideological system, but a crisis of the entire global state and political systems, new forms of nationalism flourish. When civil societies are beginning to emerge after decades or even centuries of suppression, the more sophisticated forms of Western liberal-, social- and Christian-

democratic ideologies are not easily developed. Their roots
have often proved to be much weaker than those of nationalisms rooted in historic ethnicities, which are effective vehicles
for those most ambitious for state power. The collapse of state
structures, once the underpinnings of the Cold War have been
removed, has often been swift, in a process which has spread
beyond Europe – particularly to countries such as Somalia and
Angola, former foci in Africa of East–West rivalry.

These negative effects of social forces such as ethnic
nationalisms in international relations are important to the
theoretical debate because some see their greater intrusion as
inherently destabilizing. Lawrence Freedman, for example,
could claim prophetic insight for his warning to the European
peace movements, issued more than a decade ago, that
they threatened to destabilize the international order.[13] He
expressed a concern to prevent the bipolar system being
replaced by something worse – which would lead to the world
war the peace movements themselves wished to avoid. His
argument contained the assumption that social movements
could disrupt the finely balanced relations between states,
bringing disorder into an imperfect but nevertheless ordered
system.

It is clear that in an obvious sense Freedman was right.
Complex social movements do introduce instability into inter-
state relations, not only because there are more actors, but
because the relations of social forces to conventional state
actors are generally less clearly regulated than those between
states themselves. In a more fundamental sense, however,
Freedman's approach was limited. Since the state system exists
in the context of global society, social movements of many
kinds will inevitably influence the international system, and
their actions (just like those of states) can have both positive
and negative effects. Any valid conception of world order in
the post-Cold War era must be based on more than a new set
of relations between states. It must also include civil societies in
a way which states (and international relations theorists) have
been reluctant to do in the past.

## Theoretical directions in the new global context

Earlier in this chapter we discussed how the sociological perspectives on state and society, which we examined in Chapter 2, had entered the debate in international relations. We noted, however, the tensions in this incorporation of sociology, and argued that the sociological contribution itself needed radical development. This need has been underlined by the implications of the new global and international situation, some of whose dimensions we have discussed in this chapter.

Clearly many of the concepts developed by social theorists have been of a very general character, and give us few specific directions in which to take analysis. Nevertheless their meaning for contemporary developments can generally be deduced. Mann polemically argued, for example, that 'class politics and geopolitics are separable' and the historical linkage 'between national and international class struggles can (and should) be rendered obsolete'.[14] He is dealing, however, with one sort of social input into international relations, the role of social-systemic differences. What he is referring to is the reified 'class' struggle of 'capitalism versus socialism', rather than the real class struggles of, say, Soviet miners or French farmers and the ways in which these may connect with international relations.

Debate can take place about the extent to which the end of the Cold War, like the Cold War itself, resulted from such a conflict of social systems. Halliday argues that the coincidence of the demise of communism and the end of the Cold War clearly demonstrates the 'inter-systemic' character of the conflict.[15] Thompson, in contrast, argues again for seeing the Cold War as a 'system' of relationships between adversary states – and their societies.[16] It is not hard to see the limitations of this debate: the Cold War was both a system which conditioned the existence of separate socio-economic systems in the two halves of Europe, *and* conditioned by the differences of these two systems. The extended Stalinist system of 1945–90 was, after all, a product not of social revolutions in Eastern Europe, but of geopolitics. The Soviet Union imposed its system on Eastern Europe in order to create a defensive buffer in actions which helped trigger the Cold War, and it sustained its satellites because of the Cold War. In turn, however, the social and political system of the satellites proved to be the Achilles' heel not just of the Soviet 'system' but of the Cold War 'system' as a whole. As Thompson argues, the emergence of social forces such as peace movements, opposed to both the Stalinist social system and to the Cold War international order, was of critical importance.

In a broader sense, then, Mann's argument for the separation of geopolitics and social relations cannot be sustained, and it weakens the necessary contribution of sociology to the understanding of international relations. Giddens's approach, in its apparent failure to allow for the role of social conflict in international relations, would appear at first sight to be almost as limited. The argument that what we have is a world of warring nation-states, whose administrative power is ever increasing the surveillance and pacification of societies, would not appear to be supported by the success of revolutions in breaking up the Soviet empire and the Cold War, leading to a new international unity among the states of the industrialized world.

The problem of Giddens's concepts, however, would appear to be partly their level of generality. They are simply not specific enough to deal with changes of the kind which we are discussing. It is not difficult, though, to see how his argument could be developed to take account of recent changes. The problem with the Soviet system, it could be suggested, was the insufficiently modern nature of the state. Neither the multi-national Soviet empire, nor the satellite states which each lacked a genuinely national character, were properly nation-states. Partly because of this, these states manifested a traditional rather than a modern balance between physical coercion and surveillance as means of maintaining internal order.

Military power, which according to Giddens is almost exclusively an external means of power for modern nation-states, was for the Stalinist states a vital means of suppressing social unrest (as shown by the depressingly repetitive responses to Eastern European revolts from the 1950s to the 1980s). The crude coercion of the labour camps, the political prisons and even the psychiatric wards was a long way from the sophisticated surveillance of the most advanced Western states, which is Giddens's model.

From this sort of perspective, the Eastern European revolutions and the reform-fragmentation process in the Soviet Union can be seen as transformations of modernity, assisting the consolidation of modern nation-states. 'All previous revolutions have only succeeded in building up the state machine', wrote Marx in the middle of the nineteenth century. It was also to be true, despite Marx's expectation to the contrary, of the proletarian revolution – in Russia and elsewhere. It may now be true of the 1989 revolutions in Eastern Europe, in Giddens's sense of the achievement of modern nation-states with effective administrative power leading to more balanced surveillance of societies.

This discussion highlights the ambiguities of 'surveillance' as a concept with which to grasp the relationship between society and the state. Clearly it can be read in a one-sided sense, as a new, less physically coercive but nevertheless wholly oppressive form of state power. Giddens also suggests, however, that the development of surveillance is related to democratization (as it clearly is in the extension we have made to Eastern Europe). Modern nation-states also involve a more genuine balance between society and the state, in which society is able to influence state forms. Surveillance may actually be the price of social reform, and involve the creation of institutions able to monitor social inequalities and achieve social change within the nation-state framework. 'Underprivileged groups', as Giddens argues, 'have many opportunities to actualise sources of countervailing power.'[17]

Even the peaceful revolutions of 1989 can have a place in such a Giddensian scenario. Clearly this was a moment of great tension: Leipzig, Berlin or Prague could have gone the way of Tiananmen Square. The tanks which Honecker ordered to be used, Jakes would like to have used and Ceauşescu did use against the demonstrators (before they were turned against him) could have left a much bloodier trail across Eastern Europe. The 'Velvet Revolution' was a fragile achievement, but it was achieved nonetheless, and its success is a portent. This unique moment, in which the ruled opted entirely for peaceful protest, and the rulers (thanks to Gorbachev, and excluding Romania) gave in without significant violence, is testimony to the positive side of pacification, as Giddens describes it. The achievement of fundamental political change, of a genuine revolution, without violence, is welcome confirmation of this side of the modern nation-state. That Gorbachev, in his attempt to create such a state in the Soviet Union, clearly identified the need to avoid military violence as a way of solving even such fundamental issues as the survival of communism, bears witness to the association of the modern state with pacification.

Even more interesting, from the point of view of inter-national relations, is that the Eastern European revolutions brought about not an increased danger of war but an unprecedented outbreak of peace between the major powers. Skocpol has argued that war is not external, but internal, to revolution. War is often, if not usually, a condition for revolution, and revolution in turn almost always involves war.[18]

The first side of this formula was partially met in that the militarized character of the Stalinist states was a major contributor to their downfall; they were largely the products of war, and the Cold War had helped to freeze their political forms. Military competition with the West was certainly an important part of their socio-economic crisis, just as the costs of war had weighed heavily on *ancien régime* France and Tsarist Russia (leading as Skocpol shows to their classical revolutions).

The second part of the equation was not met, however, because of the different international context in which the revolutions occurred. Classical revolutions – from the French, Russian and Chinese, which Skocpol discusses, to the Iranian (which invited, so to speak, the Iraqi invasion of 1980 and the bloodiest war of recent times), have always destabilized the international order. Instability has always equated with war. The peaceful revolutions of Eastern Europe, however, emerged from Gorbachev's project of reforming international relations, and their leaders supported this project. At the primary inter-state levels, of relations between the major powers and between the main Eastern and Western European states, these revolutions therefore accentuated rather than contradicted the development of a peaceful international order. Instability there has been in these inter-state relations, but of a kind which has been managed successfully between states.

This raises another area in which Giddens's analysis can be extended. Pacification, as Rosenberg has pointed out, is a process which pertains not only within nation-states but between them.[19] The picture of internally pacified but externally warring nation-states which Giddens presented was not fully accurate as a description of the post-war world. There was an important extension of surveillance and pacification to inter-state relations within both military blocs. Within the USA–NATO–Japan axis, and on a lesser scale within the Soviet–Eastern European bloc, war had been eliminated by the new relations of superpower domination resulting from the Second World War.

The Cold War, arms race and surveillance of lesser states were the mechanisms which kept the blocs in place, and (paradoxically) guaranteed an important degree of pacification. East–West competition also involved, as advocates of deterrence argued, the mutual surveillance of the superpowers. Although this was inherently unstable, it is arguable that the precarious international pacification which it involved never-theless paved the way for a more durable pacification of the core of state system, which is now developing. All in all, the overall picture still may have been very much as Giddens presented it, but limited international as well as domestic pacification existed within the framework of warfare.

The end of the Cold War raises the prospect of a radical extension of this process, in which surveillance ceases (especially in the East) to be a crude mechanism of superpower domination, and becomes a means of collaboration, mutual monitoring and embryonic global decision-making between somewhat more equal partners. The possibility exists of a new 'European peace order', as Booth describes it: that the whole northern industrialized world will constitute a 'security community', within which war will be as effectively eliminated as it is already within the narrower European Union, or within the old blocs.[20] This can be achieved only by a huge extension of international surveillance. The mechanisms for this are beginning to be created in the development of the United Nations and various regional security frameworks, and in the international regimes on climate control and environmental problems.

The extension of surveillance to the international level raises even more acutely the problem which has already been highlighted: that of democratization and societal inputs. As we have already seen, one fundamental danger of the new international order is a lack of equity between North and South. Another equally important danger is the exclusion of societies, of the people, from a process which is managed between states. International surveillance must become mutual, and more equal, not only between one state and another but also between state system and global society. The positive contribution of civil society to the end of the Cold War must not be an isolated moment, to be followed by a retreat from international concern which allows states to remonopolize the process. On the contrary, it should be the beginning of extended surveillance of inter-state relations by social groups, movements and parties in a developing global civil society in order to make international relations accountable to the people.

What this theoretical discourse does not take account of so far is the spread of the new wars in the former USSR and Yugoslavia. The second part of Skocpol's formula may not have been realized in wars between the major powers, or among major European states; it has been realized, however, in lesser but still very murderous and destructive wars within these former multinational states. These wars are often described simply as 'civil wars' but, in the most important cases, they have a dual aspect: inter-state wars between the successor states (Armenia–Azerbaijan, Serbia–Croatia) and civil wars between minority ethnic groups and successor states, and between communities (including plural communities as well as ethnically defined groups). Even considered as inter-state wars, the new wars, as wars for territory, are fought by the sucessor states against their own and neighbouring populations as well as against rival states. They are, in a grisly resurrection of some of the worst features of total war, wars of genocide, or, in the contemporary euphemism, 'ethnic cleansing'.

These situations certainly cast a pall over the early post-Cold War vision of a peaceful northern industrialized world, although they do not alter the transition to post-militarism which is occurring in the pacified core of global society. What these new wars emphasize is that this transition should not be as a vindication of the classical sociological theme of a peaceful industrial society, a victory of sociological utopianism over international relations realism.

This is clear when we consider the circumstances of the very partial global pacification which is occurring. The consolidation of peace is only an outcome of the most horrendous effects of the industrialization of warfare. Only the effects of two world wars, in subordinating most state rivalries within blocs, and of the nuclear arms race in forcing the recognition of the need for a global security order, have brought us precariously to the threshold of a peaceful industrial society. It has been not the automatic effects of scientific and technological or socio-economic rationality, but the twisted results of their utilization in international conflict, which have forced the issue. The social foundation of international cooperation in production, which theorists as diverse as Comte and Marx stressed, is a necessary but not a sufficient condition of peace: it requires definite state forms, at an international as well as a national level, to achieve it. The new wars emphasize how far we are from fully reaching adequate state forms on a global level.

If neither realism nor utopianism on its own offers solutions, there may be a case, as Giddens has argued, for 'utopian realism', which looks beyond the horizons of warring nation-states.[21] Such an approach, it is clear, requires an integration of sociology and international relations in understanding the relationships between societies and states. These disciplines, however, must be prepared to recognize each other's diversity. There has been a tendency, in the appropriation of sociology by international relations, to see the former as more unified than it actually is: it is to be hoped that this book conveys something of the debate within sociology which is needed to make the discipline relevant to the new international situation.

Sociologists may of course fall (indeed this essay may have done) into the parallel danger of overunifying international relations approaches. It is probably the case that sociology can provide only part of the infrastructure for a new approach to international relations; its lack of specific expertise, when it enters into the international arena, has been apparent in recent explorations. International relations theory must itself generate new synthetic approaches which do more than integrate societies in a subordinate role into a perspective centred on the state system. Rosenau's argument for a 'conceptual jailbreak' from the categories of international relations, leading to the identification of 'post-international politics' as a new object of study, is the sort of development which promises to break down the divisions between international relations, political science and sociology in studying the interaction of trans-national, national and sub-national politics.[22]

In this approach, the rigidities of both national and inter-national politics are seen as dissolving in a new flux, indeed 'turbulence', of global and societal relationships. States may survive, limping along, buffeted by internal and external forces that drive the norms, habits and practices relevant to their capacities for cooperation to the brink of transformation, and yet managing to persist, sometimes resisting the tides of change and sometimes astride them, but with few exceptions retaining sufficient legitimacy to sustain their essential structures and undertake collective action.[23]

States, then, remain central actors in world politics, but their interactions are surrounded and complemented by the ever more important interventions of transnational and sub-national actors. The argument for seeing world politics as a whole, in the context of global society, in which the 'international' is only one and an increasingly subordinate part, opens the door to a new kind of study of the global social and political system. In this conception the post-international replaces the international as the context of study, and the approach is not merely multidisciplinary, but in an important sense supradisciplinary.

## NOTES

1  The forms of this are discussed in my *Post-Military Society*, Cambridge: Polity, 1991.
2  This is essentially a development of the years 1990–3 and was only partially understood at the time of writing *Post-Military Society* (finished in early 1991).
3  Martin Shaw, ed., 'War, imperialism and the state system: a critique of orthodox Marxism for the 1980s'. In *War, State and Society*, London: Macmillan, 1984, pp. 47–70.
4  Vendulka Kubalkova and Albert Cruickshank, *Marxism-Leninism and the Theory of International Relations*, London: Routledge & Kegan Paul, 1980, and *Marxism and International Relations*, Oxford: Oxford University Press, 1985.
5  Andrew Linklater, *Beyond Realism and Marxism*, London: Macmillan, 1990.
6  See the papers in Michael Banks and Martin Shaw, eds, *State and Society in International Relations*, Hemel Hempstead: Harvester-Wheatsheaf, 1991, in which an earlier version of this chapter first appeared.
7  Fred Halliday, 'State and society in international relations'. In Banks and Shaw, *State and Society in International Relations*, pp. 191–210.
8  Skocpol, *States and Social Revolutions*, Cambridge: Cambridge University Press, 1979.
9  Mann, 'Capitalism and militarism'. In Shaw, ed., *War, State and Society*, London: Macmillan, 1984, pp. 25–46.

10   Giddens, *The Nation-State and Violence*, Cambridge: Polity, 1985.

11   Faruk Yalvaç, 'Sociology and international relations'. In Banks and Shaw, pp. 93–114.

12   Michael Cox, 'Whatever happened to the "Second Cold War": Soviet–American relations 1980–88', *Review of International Studies*, 16, 1990, pp. 158–72.

13   Lawrence Freedman, 'A criticism of the European nuclear disarmament movement', *ADIU Bulletin* (Sussex University), 4, pp. 1–3.

14   Michael Mann, 'War and social theory: into battle with classes, nations and states'. In Colin Creighton and Martin Shaw, eds, *The Sociology of War and Peace*, London: Macmillan, 1987, p. 71.

15   Fred Halliday, 'A reply to Edward Thompson', *New Left Review*, 182, 1990, pp. 147–51.

16   E. P. Thompson, 'The end of the Cold War', *New Left Review*, 182, 1990, pp. 139–46.

17   Anthony Giddens, 'Modernity and utopia', *New Statesman and Society*, 2 November 1990, p. 22.

18   Skocpol, *States and Social Revolutions*.

19   Justin Rosenberg, 'A non-realist theory of sovereignty: Giddens' *The Nation-State and Violence*', *Millenium*, 19, 1990, pp. 249–70.

20   Ken Booth, 'Steps towards stable peace in Europe: a theory and practice of coexistence', *International Affairs*, 66, 1990, pp. 17–46.

21   Giddens, 'Modernity and utopia', p. 22.

22   James N. Rosenau, *Turbulence and World Politics*, Princeton: Princeton University Press, 1990.

23   Rosenau, p. 132.

PART THREE

# The Sociological Critique of
# International Relations

# Four

# 'There is No Such Thing as Society': Beyond the Individualism/Statism Dilemma in International Relations

If international theorists are to make the 'post-international' leap and contribute to the understanding of global politics in the context of global society, fundamental shifts of theoretical perspective are essential. The most important of these focus on the relations of state, state system and society. In this and the following chapter we explore the implications of the absence, or at best the weakness, of a concept of society in international theory, and the use of a misplaced concept of 'international society' which follows from a statist conception.

This chapter explores these issues by offering a critical sociological perspective on a key conceptual issue in international relations, the question of security. Within international political theory, one of the most fundamental signs of rethinking has been a reworking of the concept of security. As Ken Booth has put it, 'The last decade or so has seen a growing unease with the traditional concept of security, which privileges the state and emphasizes military power' together with 'a frequent call for a "broadening" or "updating" of the concept of security'.[1] The end of the Cold War has undoubtedly greatly reinforced the critical tendencies, so that it is now possible to discuss West European security, for example, in largely (but alas not wholly) non-military terms, with reference to non-violence, democracy and human

righst, population movements, economic relations and environmental issues.[2]

One of the first texts in international studies to argue
comprehensively for this wider view of security was Barry
Buzan's *People, States and Fear*.[3] For many, as Smith notes,
'the book marked a real breakthrough in the literature,
broadening and deepening the concept of security in a way that
opened up the whole subject area as never before.'[4] For Booth,
it is still 'the most comprehensive analysis of the concept in
international relations literature to date'.[5]

Despite this praise, both these writers oppose Buzan on the
definition of security. Booth asserts that *People, States and
Fear* 'can primarily be read as an explanation of the difficulties
surrounding the concept. The book not only argues that
security is an "essentially contested concept" defying pursuit of
an agreed definition, but asserts that there is not much point
struggling to make it uncontested.' Such a conclusion, Booth
argues correctly, is 'unsatisfying': 'If we cannot name it, how
can we hope to achieve it?'[6] Insofar as Buzan does commit
himself, both Booth and Smith see him as overprivileging the
state, and propose instead an *individual*-centred focus for
security studies. In this chapter, it is argued that, while security
is indeed something which appertains to individual human
beings rather than states, it is mediated not just by inter-state
relations but by the whole complex of social relations in which
they are involved.

It is argued therefore that a critical sociological approach to
understanding the concept of security can help to illuminate
the debate which is developing within international studies. I
proceed in four stages. The first section examines Buzan's
discussion of security, demonstrating how, despite its undoubted broadening of the agenda of security studies, his work
does indeed remain excessively state-bound.

The second part discusses Booth's and Smith's critical
comments on Buzan, and argues that they share with him a
common sociological weakness which ultimately undermines
the coherence of their conclusions on the crucial issue of state
*versus* individual-centred definitions of the concept. I argue

that, despite the welcome extension of the *issue* agenda of security studies to include a wide range of non-military factors, its *conceptual* framework requires more radical revision than is provided by either side of this dispute. What is needed, it is suggested, is a *deepening* as well as a *broadening* of the agenda. The concept of 'social relations' (or 'society') needs to be interposed between and around the terms 'state' and 'individual' within which the debate has been conducted.

The third part examines a novel attempt to interpose a concept of 'society' into the international security debate, in Ole Wæver's essay on 'societal security' in a recent collaboration with Buzan. While this is undoubtedly an advance, it is suggested that the concept of 'society' used is too narrowly ethnically and nationally defined, and that this apparent breakthrough therefore shares many of the weaknesses of Buzan's text.

Finally, I examine recent work by Giddens on risk and security, which suggests the nature and relevance of a sociological approach, although it does not refer to specifically international issues. In conclusion, I try to make the connections between this sociology and the international security studies debate, and suggest the basis on which a more adequate theoretical resolution can be achieved.

## A statist conception of security studies

I begin by examining the conception of security which is offered by Buzan. I shall concentrate to a large extent on the more general issues of the meaning and referents of security, and the role of the state, which in Buzan occupy the first three chapters. I shall try to show that the broadened concept of security he offers is still fundamentally a statist one which suffers from central contradictions in its understanding of the state–society relationship, and is in this sense sociologically inadequate.

*People, States and Fear* starts from the assumption that there are three levels of security, 'individual', 'national' and 'international', and notes that concepts of 'national' security have tended to organize the other two levels.[7] (This is true enough within the international relations literature; but there are many other fields within the social sciences in which the concept of security is used primarily to refer to the individual or other sub-state levels: I shall return to the implications of this below.) Buzan further notes the historic 'militarization' of the concept to which this pattern generally gave rise, and the growing criticism of this notion of security 'bound to the level of individual states and military issues', which as Buzan points out is 'inherently inadequate'.[8] This criticism within international relations resulted, however, according to Buzan's account, more in an emphasis on the interdependence of international security relations – and thus in a resort to the 'international' level – as in a turning to the level of 'individual' security.[9]

Buzan uses the term 'the security of human collectivities', but, viewing things from the standpoint of the international system, he assumes that one particular sort of institution is 'the standard unit of security'. This institution is 'the sovereign territorial state'. It seems Buzan regards the state as itself a type of 'collectivity', but the state is also an institution linked to another basic type of collectivity, the nation. Ideally, however, these two go together. 'The ideal type is the nation-state, where ethnic and cultural boundaries line up with political ones . . . . But since nation and states do not fit neatly together in many places, non-state collectivities, particularly nations, are also an important unit of analysis.'[10]

This analysis leaves us with two crucial problems which are inadequately resolved, if at all. An absolutely critical issue, but one which amazingly is not fully clarified, is whether 'national security' refers primarily to the nation or to the state; ideally, of course, these are symbiotically linked, but what happens where they are not? To continue to use the language of 'national' security implies, if it reflects more than terminological inexactness or conservatism, a preference for nations. Buzan recognizes this in writing that 'national security implies strongly that the object of security is the nation'.[11]

A difficulty of this line of argument is that it places a large onus on the concept of 'nation': however, Buzan, like most international theorists, barely defines the term, which does not even figure in his index. Certainly 'nation' is difficult, arguably much more so than 'state', but that very fact places a greater responsibility on the theorist – if he wishes to make 'nation' so central – to achieve at least some working definition, or explain, like Mayall, why he does not impose a single definition.[12]

In any case, Buzan's position is that 'the standard unit of security is . . . the sovereign territorial state' and so ultimately he abandons a consistently national concept. He argues, indeed, that 'national security in the strict sense is a concept with only limited application to the state.'[13]

Although Buzan examines some of the complexity of state–nation relationships, he does not resolve the lack of conceptual clarity on the nation long characteristic of international relations theory.[14] One could argue that a serious attempt to tackle this issue cannot really be achieved without an exploration of society and culture, but these are fields which Buzan does not enter. The sociological literature would lead us to see nations as cultural-ideological-political constructs – 'imagined communities' in Anderson's term[15] – rather than 'real' social collectivities in some prior objective sense (although one should not doubt the reality of culture, ideology or politics). In this context, the relation between nation and state is intrinsically, rather than contingently, contradictory and problematic, so that any attempt to build a concept of security on its shifting sands is brought very severely into question.

The more fundamental problem which is revealed is that of the nature of human collectivities in general. Buzan's formulation certainly admits of the possibility that there may be other types of human collectivity than the nation-state/nation/ethnic group, to which security issues may be attached. No other type is actually indicated, however, in his discussion. A reference to 'ethno-cultural units', coupled with a definition of 'societal security' in terms of the sustainability of 'traditional patterns of language, culture and religious and national identity and custom',[16] suggests that the only sorts of 'human collectivities' which are being admitted to theoretically significant status are those which approximate the basis for a nation-state. Those formed on axes other than ethnicity/nationality – on gender, class, community or lifestyle lines, for example – are not in practice considered relevant, although it may be argued that they are just as capable of generating 'security' concerns. Again, there is a good deal to suggest that, while *formally* flexible, the conception is in practice tied closely to state-centred definitions of 'national' security.

Buzan stresses that his definition of the field of 'international security studies' is intended to leave it broader than that of 'strategic studies', seen as more narrowly tied to military power. He lists five major factors in 'the security of human collectives', military, political, economic, societal (as defined above) and environmental. However, it is clear from the above that broadening the *issue*-agenda of security studies from the military-strategic dimension does not necessarily involve broadening the *conceptual* base. The recognition of additional dimensions of security – however welcome this may be – may be an *ad hoc* enlargement of a still state-centred concept of security.

This critique may sound paradoxical in view of Buzan's explicit contention that 'security has many potential referent objects', and that to identify security with the state ignores the 'amorphous multi-faceted' nature of the state as a 'collective object' and the multiplicity of states which means that 'the security of one cannot be discussed without reference to the others'.[17] It is not clear, however, that these statements function as anything more than *caveats* to a state-centred notion of security – complex qualifications which in the end preserve the integrity of the project more or less intact. What finally inclines me to this view is that, by defining the issue of security in terms of three levels, of which 'individuals' are the only sub-national/state level, Buzan has effectively ruled out any referents other than states or quasi-state collectivities as a serious basis for security studies.

Buzan's discussion of individual security opens with the

statement that 'the idea of security is easier to apply to things than to people' (p. 35). This is curious because the things in question (money, material goods) have meaning only in relation to the people who own or use them. Their 'security' really means (as Buzan states in parentheses) 'their owners' security in possession of them'. In this sense we cannot talk at all of the 'security of things' as opposed to the 'security of individuals'.

Buzan seems to be trying to ascribe to individual security a particularly nebulous character when he writes that

> Different aspects of individual security are frequently contradictory (protection from crime versus erosion of civil liberties) and plagued by the difficulty of distinguishing between objective and subjective evaluation. Cause–effect relationships with regard to threats are often obscure and controversial (individual versus social explanations for crime). (p. 36)

Each of these statements is at least equally true, however, of 'national security' – indeed, as we have seen, it is not possible to determine at a theoretical level, within Buzan's text, exactly what is the 'referent' of national security (nation, state, or nation-state). This is a difficulty which we do not have in quite the same way with individual security.

Individual security seems to be important for Buzan principally in that it provides a basis for national security. Freedom for one individual, in a predictably Hobbesian scenario, may be an actual or potential threat to the security of others, and the problem is how to balance freedom and security. The state is justified as an instrument for achieving this balance, and thus national security can be seen, to some extent, as individual security writ large: 'The security of individuals is inseparably entangled with that of the state' (p. 39). 'State and society become increasingly indistinguishable,' adds Buzan (p. 39), in a phrase which recalls – and compounds – the conceptual confusion over nation and state which we noted earlier.

Buzan recognizes the possible contradictions between the requirements of state and individual security, when 'the state becomes a major source of threat to its citizens' (p. 39), but he loses this point in a discussion about the 'maximalist' and 'minimalist' views of the state, defined as seeing the state as, respectively, greater than the sum of its (individual) parts, and reducible to those parts. The issue is muddled still further by an attempt to distinguish between different states as 'maximal' or 'minimal' (in which it seems to be suggested that it is principally 'maximal' states which threaten their citizens). This argument is confusing because 'maximalist' and 'minimalist' views are surely concepts of the state in general, their validity not related to whether we can distinguish between different types of state.

This whole debate suffers from the misplaced abstraction which bedevils political theory, according to which individuals are conceived, not within the context of their social relations in general, but as members of a particular institution, the nation-state;[18] and, conversely, states are conceived not as the conglomerates of institutions which they really are, embedded in complex social relations, but as constructed on the basis of a notional contract with individual citizens.

Nevertheless, Buzan proceeds to provide us with a useful summary of the ways in which, even in democratic states, 'the individual citizen faces many threats which emanate directly or indirectly from the state.'[19] And he argues that

> just as there is a very mixed set of costs and benefits to individual security in relation to the state's civil order functions, so is there for its external security functions. The state is supposed to provide a measure of protection to its citizens from foreign interference, attack and invasion. But it cannot do so without imposing risks and costs on them. . . . While the principle may be firmly rooted, however, the practice which develops around it can easily become an intense source of dispute on the grounds of individual versus national security. . . . Modern war is known to produce high risks and high casualties, and this makes decisions about what constitutes a threat to the security of the state a matter of considerable public concern.[20]

Nuclear weapons obviously raise this contradiction in a particularly acute form, as Buzan shows.

This presentation of the conflicting requirements of individual and state security does not prevent Buzan from according them different theoretical priorities. He concludes that 'individual security . . . is essentially subordinate to the higher-level political structures of the state and international system', and that 'because this is so, national and international security cannot be reduced to individual security.'[21] Individuals are mainly to be considered because of the way in which, in pursuing their own security, they may influence the higher levels of national or international security.

It is in discussing national security and the state as such that Buzan most clearly makes explicit the issues which have been troubling us so far. He starts from the premise that 'the state is composed of individuals bound together in a collective political unit',[22] which reflects the normative conception of political theory and dismisses the 'rather inward-looking perspectives of Political Science and Sociology'.[23] We may agree about 'inward-lookingness', if by that is meant the tendency to define the state principally in relation to the social structure *within* the territory of the state. (But it should be noted that this is precisely what recent sociological theorists have rejected.)

There is, however, a much more fundamental issue, expressed by Buzan in references to what he calls 'the definition of the state in Weberian terms, where state and society are viewed as separate phenomena, and the state is seen almost entirely in politico-institutional terms'; and to how such 'narrow' definitions are reinforced by 'Marxian thinking, which also stresses the separation of government and society'. 'Although this perspective has its uses', Buzan concludes, 'it is much too narrow to serve as a basis for thinking about security. . . . The reduction of "state" to mean simply the institutions of central government does not work at the international level.'[24]

I had to stop myself from putting 'sic' after that use of the word 'narrow' in the last quotation. While I suppose that a view that defines the state as distinct from society can be described as as a 'narrow' view of the state – in that it doesn't incorporate the whole of society into the concept of state – the opposite view, which Buzan advances, is certainly a very narrow view of society – it refuses to acknowledge autonomous social relations as a factor in international relations distinct from the state, and incorporates society into international theory only as an adjunct of the state.

It is not only Weberians, or Marxists, but sociologists in general who cannot but protest at this mind-boggling denial of the significance of *social relations in general*. There is a fundamental conceptual and historical point at issue here. Human beings entered into social relations of various kinds before they began to develop states. States are only one kind of human institution. The relations between states and societies have undergone immense change throughout human history and are continuing to do so. The semi-identity between nation-states and national societies which has characterized the twentieth century is historically novel, currently problematic, and not likely to survive in the form which is assumed by much international theory. From the point of view of sociology, to object to an analytical separation of state and society is to deny oneself the tools with which to analyse the role of states in the modern world.

In this discussion we are using 'society' as a term to refer to the concept of social relations in general, rather than in the sense of a fixed unit of social organization. Although it may be the case that in the past there have been such units which have existed in complete or near-complete isolation from one another, it is clear, as we suggested in Chapter 1, that in the modern world this is no longer the case. If we wish to talk of 'a' society, we can probably do so only at a global level. 'Societies' in the sense of tribal, ethnic, national or state-bound units are no more than reflections of attempts to define, partially, and more or less arbitrarily, the separateness of certain groups within the global flux of social relations. While this sort of usage may be acceptable (even unavoidable) as a shorthand way of describing social realities, it is utimately of limited theoretical value. Again, it is not such usage which is referred to here, but 'society' in the sense of social relations in general.

Buzan lacks such a general concept of society; indeed if he has a concept of society, it is clearly of societies as the domestic fields of states, that is, of state-bound segments of social relations. This enters into the argument as a critique of 'the traditional International Relations view of the state as a political-territorial billiard ball' as 'also too restrictive'. He states that 'security issues within an international anarchy are highly conditioned not only by the structure of the system and by the interactions of states, but also by the domestic characteristics of states. Consequently, security analysis requires a comprehensive definition of the state which combines both of these perspectives.'[25]

So far so good, but the levels of society cannot be reduced to their influence on the 'domestic characteristics of states', that is, be admitted to the discussion only as an appendage to the level of states on which the discussion is focused. The unity of state and society is precisely what cannot and should not be assumed in any analysis of the state or of international relations.

Buzan clearly regards his distinction of 'strong' and 'weak' states, from which he draws major conclusions for security, as a manifestation of this recognition of society.[26] As a classification of states, it obviously has considerable value: strong states, with greater socio-political cohesion, are more capable of providing certain sorts of security to society within their territories, while weak states, with poorer socio-political cohesion, are less capable. The analysis has been vindicated by the collapse of the Soviet Union, described as 'having serious weaknesses' as a state, even though a great power:[27] the resulting tensions have increased security for individuals and groups of all kinds in its former territory, at many levels.

Although this discussion suggests ways in which social organization may have consequences for state cohesion and security, it still considers society only as an aspect of state organization. This is, moreover, the highpoint of Buzan's discussion of the state and society. The difficulties for his approach of dealing with sociological concepts is demonstrated further by a curious discussion of the comparability of individual and state as 'objects' (not as actors) and 'referents' of security.[28] At no point in this does Buzan show any recognition that his problem – the nature of a collective or institutional social form (or actor?) in contrast to an individual – is a general sociological problem which applies to human groups and institutions of all kinds, and not just to states.

Buzan's approach is, it appears, irredeemably state-centred. He certainly recognizes the complexities of the state, but he fails to locate it in an adequate sociological context. Because he counterposes only individuals to states, and because the only social groups which are genuinely admitted to his discussion are state-oriented collectivities (nations, ethnic groups), his concept of security prioritizes national (and by extension, international) over individual security, generates no general concept of 'social' security, and leaves us with a notion of security centred on the manifoldly problematic notion of 'national security'.

Although there are approaches within international relations which may not share its deficiencies, Buzan's work can clearly stand as largely typical. As Booth points out, there have been surprisingly few attempts to define 'security', and Buzan's *modus operandi* approach has the important merits of attempting to unravel concepts which most writers simply assume. What is more, it can be suggested that even those who disagree with Buzan's conclusions share much of his conceptual approach. It is significant that even Booth's powerful 'emancipatory' plea falls largely under this stricture.

## Individualism: an inadequate basis for anti-statism

Critics of Buzan's statism from within international studies have largely counterposed to it an 'individualist' perspective. For Smith, the question of 'security for whom' is highly problematic in Buzan's work: 'the worry persists that he sees states as ontologically prior to other candidates. As a result the state gets undertheorised and privileged.' The alternative is that 'there is a strong case for placing individuals, not states, at the centre of security studies, which would result in a rather different conceptual focus.'[29]

It is Booth who has most clearly developed the 'individualist' case against Buzan. He starts from the very important rejection of states as 'the primary referent objects of security'. He argues this on three grounds: that states 'are unreliable as primary referents because whereas some are in the business of security (internal and external) some are not'; that 'it is illogical to place states at the centre of our thinking about security because even those which are the producers of security . . . represent the means and not the ends' (rather, he says, as a house is to its inhabitants: it is the latter's security which is primary); and because states are 'too diverse in character to serve as the basis for a comprehensive theory of security.'[30] Of these objections, clearly the second is foremost. Booth's rejection of *People, States and Fear* is based on the 'litmus test' of the primary referent: 'is it states, or is it people? Whose security comes first? I want to argue, following the World Society School, buttressed on this point by Hedley Bull, that individual humans are the ultimate referent'.[31]

Both the content and form of this argument are interesting. Booth poses the question in very much the same way as Buzan, individual *versus* state: the difference between them lies in the answer. Empirically, he gives some pointers to the relation of individuals and states by mentioning as examples of struggles for emancipation not only 'the struggle for freedom of the colonial world', but also 'women, youth, the proletariat, appetites of all sorts, homosexuals, consumers, and thought'.[32] No more, however, than Buzan does Booth offer, in his critique of the former, any concepts or levels of analysis either to *explain* the relationship between individual and state, or to stand *between* them. At the same time, it is noteworthy that Booth's secondary arguments, on the unreliability (from a security point of view) and diversity of states, are points also made by Buzan and readily (for the most part) accommodated within his framework. It also seems significant that Booth buttresses his individualism only with references to theorists within international relations, rather than in wider philosophical or methodological terms.

There is, of course, a much larger debate on this issue, which concerns much more than the state and is central to the social sciences as a whole. The postulate of 'methodological individualism' – according to which it is assumed that individuals are the subjects of social action – was advanced by Weber,[33] in opposition to holistic and organicist sociologies. Buzan's discussion indicates that organic analogies between the human individual and the state are still troubling international relations, and indeed recent linguistic analysis of the concept of 'security' suggests the deeply organic roots of the literature.[34]

Individualism belongs, moreover, to a perspective in which social science is concerned not with 'objects' but with 'action'. Collective action, ascribed to social groups or to institutions, is ultimately to be understood in terms of, but not necessarily or immediately reduced to, the actions of individuals. In practice social scientists are very much concerned with social groups and institutions, but we need to be aware of the abstraction necessary to analyse social life in these terms, and avoid endowing these social forms with characteristics which can only belong to individuals.

The relevance of this argument to the present discussion is that it indicates not just that we *should* be concerned, as Booth argues, with individual above state security, but that, even when we talk about state security, we are ultimately talking about an institution constructed by human beings and which involves individuals in many ways. We cannot, from a methodological point of view, simply assume the fiction of political theory according to which states represent their citizens in a general sense. We have to examine the particular connections which individual members of society (we cannot simply consider them as citizens) – both those involved in running the state and those 'outside' it – really have with the state.

In practice, again, this must involve additional levels of analysis. We cannot, as a matter of practical social knowledge, examine even the individual roles of all the members of a government – let alone of all those involved in the state machine, let alone of all those in society at large who have some relationship with the state. We are forced to make assumptions about social groupings of various kinds, through which individuals act, and which interpose between individuals and the state.

In this sense, when we discuss security, it is not just a question of the security of individuals *versus* that of the state, but of a complex, multilayered analysis, in which the security of individuals may be a starting place, but in which we have to examine security issues which affect social groups (below the state level) as well as issues of state security. We also have to examine the roles of individuals in relation to group and state issues, and of social groups and states in relation to individual issues, as well as of states in relation to individual and group issues. In reality even this conception is highly simplified, since I am using the term 'social groups' to cover an enormous range of ways in which individuals are involved in social relations.

All this discussion points to the fact that social relations (or 'society') is the missing dimension of the security debate. 'There is no such thing as society', Margaret Thatcher is reported to have said, and it seems as though international relations theorists, including some who would doubtless abhor her company, have fallen into a parallel theoretical trap. 'Society', however, is, as we have indicated above, best regarded as a codeword for the complex of *social relations in general*, which form the fundamental context of individual and state activity, rather than a fixed entity or even a level of analysis. There is indeed 'no such thing as society', if by society we mean a specific structure which determines all else: thus 'British society' and similar concepts denote (as we have indicated) not fixed realities but partial – and more or less useful – abstractions from the flux of social life. Society in the generic sense, of the social relations between human individuals which are represented in constantly changing ways in the range of social groups and institutions, is, however, not merely a but *the* reality within which alone it makes sense to look at the relations of institutions such as states.[35]

In another recent work, Booth has himself advanced a more sociological view, in his proposal that the concept of 'communities' should be a guiding concept of a new, more human international relations. He outlines the prospect of a 'new medievalism' based on the replacement of the 'anarchical society' of states by a 'community of communities'.[36] This concept of community is an important step beyond the individualism of his critique of Buzan. 'Community' functions, however, primarily as a normative rather than an analytical concept. Booth discusses some instances of community, such as the moral union of the French and German peoples which underlies the peace between them, and he mentions some principles, such as multiculturality, but he does not give any systematic suggestions about how communities are (or are to be) formed, or enter (or should enter) into world politics.

The proposal of 'communities' raises, therefore, the same sociological questions: on the basis of which sorts of social relationships (on what 'social bases') are communities being, or to be, constructed? If communities are no longer constructed, in Buzan's quasi-realist terms, simply or mainly on the basis of nationality or ethnicity – and there is of course a lot of impressive evidence that these are still important axes – what are the social bases of inter- or supranationalism? Class, morality, culture? While it is possible and desirable for international and social theorists to identify with the 'human community' in general, the realization of Booth's goals depends on the construction of human *communities* based on specific social relations. We need a fuller working out of the suggestive examples of a 'utopian' approach. Here a more developed sociology, as advocated in this critique, is essential.

## 'Societal security': a critique of Wæver

A novel approach which promises just such a sociological attitude towards security is Wæver's essay on 'societal security'.[37] Wæver first defines 'society', and uses Giddens to make a distinction, similar to that proposed in Chapter 1 of this book, between society 'in the generalised connotation of "social association" or interaction', and in the sense of 'a society' as 'a unity, having boundaries which mark it off from other, surrounding societies'.[38] Unfortunately, at this point Wæver not only rejects Giddens's insistence on the priority of the first concept, and dismisses the idea of global society in one sentence; he also limits his interest baldly to 'societies as units operating in an international system', thus tying the definition of 'societies' directly to what is, in reality, the system of states. 'We need a separate concept of society (and nation) to operate in parallel to but distinct from the state.' Wæver argues that historically the concept of society has grown up as the 'other' of the state.[39]

Although Wæver recognizes that to directly identify a given society automatically with a given state would lead to a concept of societal security which is 'at best a useless repetition of the whole argument around state security', he is determined to limit his discussion to 'societies as units'. 'How can one differentiate', he asks, 'between the security of groups in society and the security of society as a whole?'[40] It is this determination to tie himself to a concept of 'society as a whole' which is most limiting in Wæver's approach. As in Buzan's discussion quoted above, it leads to a debilitating narrowing of the concern for human security.

Wæver moves rapidly towards a conclusion similar to Buzan's, albeit by a more sophisticated route. Firstly, he cites R. B. J. Walker's emphasis on 'the extent to which the meaning of security is tied to historically specific forms of political community,'[41] and then argues that 'the main process at the present is a very open and contradictory articulation of the relationship between state (and other political structures) and nation (and other large-scale cultural communities), and therefore the main dynamic of security will play at the interface of state security and societal security (in the sense of the security of large-scale "we" identities).' The qualifications in parentheses rapidly appear to have minimal importance, as Wæver moves towards a focus on the nation 'as a special case of society' characterized by territoriality, continuity across time, and 'a feeling of being one of the units of which the global society exists' (he does not consider that one might feel this through other sorts of unit).[42]

The next step is to point out that, 'while ethno-national communities are not automatically or necessarily the prime basis for society', the only rival principle of identity with comparable strength is religion. Therefore, Wæver concludes, 'the main units of analysis for societal security are politically significant ethno-national and religious identities.'[43] The focus of study is therefore national communities, whether connected to an existing nation-state or not, and security studies concern, as already indicated, the 'interface' between societal and state security – or, alternatively, between the security of nations as communities and the 'national security' which is really the security of states.

This is not an unimportant distinction, but as a conclusion it squanders the potential of a more broadly based concept of security tied to an equally broad concept of society. Its limits can be seen quite clearly in its application to the conflict in former Yugoslavia, attempted in the same volume by Hakan Wiberg.[44] His clear and careful exposition lays bare the complex ethnic and national dimensions of the conflict and relates them to the conflicts of states. Its weakness, however, is that in accomplishing this level of analysis it omits others, and thereby accepts an ethnic nationalist interpretation of events. Except descriptively, this sort of analysis cannot deal with levels such as the security of individuals; of women as women; of couples and families; of mixed-ethnic groupings; and of those who refuse or downgrade ethno-national identities in favour of pluralist ideals (except that these can be described as residual Yugoslavs or Bosnians).

The fundamental flaw of this approach is that it defines away what are precisely the most crucial questions in ex-Yugoslavia: how is it that ethno-national identities (whose historic import-ance no one doubts, but which had been subsumed in complex processes of cultural and political integration) have come to dominate once more? Why have other forms of identity been

marginalized and defeated? What are the future relationships between ethno-national and other (especially pluralist)
identities in ex-Yugoslavia? Equally importantly, how are the
relations of the apparently triumphant ethnic nationalisms (of
the Serbians and Croatians) with the pluralist ideals of
European and global society to be negotiated in the future?

Even from within the 'societal' standpoint which Wæver
advocates, there is something paradoxical about describing the
various ethnic groups in Bosnia-Herzegovina and other regions
of ex-Yugoslavia as separate societies. Before the break-up of
the Yugoslav state and the consequent wars began, most
analysts would have agreed in describing a single Yugoslav
society, albeit with complex national, ethnic and other cultural
divisions. Even if they preferred to describe Yugoslavia in
terms of the various republics, no one could seriously have
argued that there existed separate Serb, Croat and Muslim
'societies' in Bosnia-Herzegovina. By accepting ethnic-nationalist
descriptions at face value, this approach assumes precisely
what needs to be explained: the disintegration of a largely
multi-ethnic and in some senses pluralist society into ethnic
fragments.

A sociologically adequate concept of security, applied to this
context, will subsume Wæver's 'societal' (or ethno-national)
dimension in a broader approach – closer to Booth's vision of
manifold communities – which integrates the dimensions of
individual, gender, family, local community, city, profession,
pluralist nation, Europeanism and globalism – all of which
have been violated and threatened, in the name of ethnic
nationalisms, in the ex-Yugoslav wars.


## A sociological approach to the problem of security


It will be seen, therefore, that even introducing a concept of
'societal security' into the analysis of international relations,
while undoubtedly an advance, does not in itself resolve the
difficulties of the state-biased approach of the discipline. It

is necessary to do more than recast the language of security in sociological terms; it is necessary to carry out a radical reconstruction of concepts.

It is important to ask, therefore, whether sociology (including related social sciences such as social anthropology and social policy) has anything directly to offer in terms of this project. The answer, until recently, might have been that there are a number of empirical areas in which, contrary to Buzan, considerable advances – arguably at least as great as those of international relations – have been made in defining and even measuring risk and the concomitant requirements of security for individuals and social groups. One could instance not only criminology – which is an obvious parallel[45] – but also health, traffic and of course disaster studies, not to mention the very precise actuarial assessments of risk made by accountants for insurance purposes.

Until recently there was little mainstream theoretical recognition of the problem of security. This has now been remedied, however, notably in two books by Anthony Giddens, which should be as required reading on security as his *Nation-State and Violence* has already become for thinking about the state. Giddens discusses security and risk in terms of a fundamental conceptualization of modern society, bringing the ideas to the centre of the discipline. He has a lot to say about the implications of globalization for security, but little specifically about 'international security'. In this discussion I shall attempt a brief exposition, followed by a conclusion in which I draw together the argument and attempt to make it relevant to security in an international relations context.

Giddens's argument was first elaborated, rather briefly, in an interconnected series of lectures published as *The Consequences of Modernity*. In this he makes 'security versus danger and risk versus trust' major themes of discussion. He sees modernity – the spread of modern social institutions based on abstract systems of knowledge – as double-edged: it has 'created vastly greater opportunities for human beings to enjoy a secure and rewarding existence than any pre-modern system', but it also has a 'sombre side' symbolized by war.[46]

Giddens links the concept of 'risk' closely with that of 'security', and he argues that the nature of risk has changed. There is a 'globalization of risk in the sense of intensity' (for example, nuclear war) and in terms of 'the expanding number of contingent events which affect everyone or at least very large numbers of people on the planet' (for example, changes in the global division of labour). New risks arise from the nature of modern social organization: there is risk 'stemming from the created environment, or socialized nature: the infusion of human knowledge into the material environment, and the development of 'institutionalized risk environments affecting the life-chances of millions' (for example, investment markets). In addition, and very importantly, there is greater 'awareness of risk as risk', well distributed throughout society, and incapable of being converted into certainties by religious or magic ideas.[47]

In the following work, *Modernity and Self-Identity*, Giddens provides what could be described, in terms of Buzan's discussion, as a sociological text on the individual level of security. He argues that, in conditions of modernity, individuals face not merely empirical threats of the kind noted by Buzan, but something much more fundamental. Daily life is forever reconstituted by the operation of a bewildering array of what Giddens calls 'abstract systems', knowledge-based patterns of social behaviour, coordinated through markets as well as bureaucracies, which govern the conditions of individual existence. The spread of these systems is global: 'In high modernity, the influence of distant happenings on proximate events, and on the intimacies of the self, becomes more and more commonplace.'[48] The security 'threat' which individuals face is, at base, the threat to their very identity from the ways in which abstract systems operate. The challenge to individuals is to construct and reconstruct their own identity, which is no longer given for them by traditional institutions and cultures.

Individual identities, faced with a great variety of competing and changing social contexts determined by these new realities, are constantly at risk. Giddens discusses the dangers of disruption of ontological security experienced, in consequence, by individuals in modern society, and the ways in which individuals can develop their own 'trajectories' through therapy, choice of lifestyle and development of 'life plans'.[49]

Giddens argues that 'the notion of risk is central in a society which is taking leave of the past, of traditional ways of doing things, and which is opening itself up to a problematic future.' Control of risk is an essential part of the operation of abstract systems: 'all action . . . is in principle "calculable" in terms of risk – some sort of assessment of likely risks can be made for virtually all habits and activities, in respect of specific outcomes. The intrusion of abstract systems into everyday life, coupled with the dynamic diffusion of knowledge, means that an awareness of risk seeps into the actions of almost everyone.'[50] 'Risk assessment' is an essential component of the 'colonization of the future' which is central to modernity.

Giddens argues that there has been a huge historical transformation of the nature of risk – and security.

> Preoccupation with risk in modern social life has nothing to do with the actual prevalence of life-threatening dangers. On the level of the individual life-span, in terms of life expectation and degree of freedom from serious disease, people in the developed societies are in a much more secure position than were most in previous ages.

An impressive lists follows of the ways in which the physical security of human beings has been enhanced in industrial societies; but it is counter-balanced by a list of new risks: war, motor accidents, drugs, environmental pollution, etc. Both can be seen as results of the operation of the abstract systems of modernity. 'In terms of basic life security, nonetheless', Giddens concludes, 'the risk-reducing elements seem substantially to outweigh the new array of risks.'[51]

The 'institutionalization of risk' is seen as a fundamental characteristic of the new role of risk in modern society.' A significant part of expert thinking and public discourse today is made up of *risk profiling* – analysing what, in the current state of knowledge and in current conditions, is the distribution of risk in given milieux of action.'[52]

Giddens distinguishes between 'low-' and 'high-consequence' risks: the former potentially within the control of the individual agent (for example, peculiarities of diet which may have certain medical consequences), the latter 'by definition ... remote from the individual agent, although – again by definition – they impinge directly on each individual's life-chances.'[53] Examples of high-consequence risks range from mercury in tuna fish to, at the most 'calamitous', the nuclear accident at Chernobyl. Risk assessment is a complex and constantly changing affair even in the case of low-consequence risks; it becomes highly speculative in the context of the larger high-consequence issues.

The pervasiveness of risk, Giddens repeats, is not because life is now inherently more risky.

> It is rather that, in conditions of modernity, for lay actors as well as for experts in specific fields, thinking in terms of risk and risk-assessment is a more or less ever-present expertise, of a partly imponderable character. It should be remembered that we are all laypeople in repsect of the vast majority of the expert systems which intrude on our daily activities. ... The risk climate of modernity is thus unsettling for everyone; no one escapes.

Nevertheless, 'thinking in terms of risk ... is also a means of seeking to stabilise outcomes, a mode of colonising the future.'[54]

Substantively, Giddens argues, 'the abstract systems of modernity create large areas of relative security for the continuance of everyday life' but 'the wholesale penetration of abstract systems into everyday life creates risks which the individual is not well-placed to confront.... Greater interdependence, up to and including globally interdependent systems, means greater vulnerability when untoward events occur that affect these systems as a whole.'[55] At the limit, hypothetical events such as the breakdown of the global monetary system, or global warming (let alone nuclear war), indicate the dangers. Real socially created disasters, such as the effects of the destruction of water and electricity systems in Iraq during the Gulf War, demonstrate the vulnerability of modern societies.

A problematic dimension of Giddens's discussion is that he gives little attention to the role of social groups in the distribution and negotiation of risk. It is ironic, from the point of view of this paper, that, rather as Buzan and Booth counterpose individual and state (ignoring society), Giddens appears to counterpose the individual to society and social relations in the most general sense (with little to say, in this volume, about social groups – or the state). Giddens does, however, enter an early caveat about the role of social inequalities in the distribution of risk; and, whereas Buzan attempts a general account of security as a concept, Giddens's aim is rather different, to examine the consequences of modernity for the individual.

The one area of Giddens's discussion where he does implicitly explore the dimensions of collective human action is in his final chapter, 'The Emergence of Life Politics'. Giddens's account of risk and security is clearly activist in its implications: for all the determining character of abstract systems, he does not believe that they leave people powerless. On the contrary, individuals have choices of lifestyle and life-plan. Social groups, *The Consequences of Modernity* makes clear, have the power to contest and organize around the axes of the modern social order. Giddens, interestingly, organizes his political perspective around the concept of 'utopian realism', using the term in a way which is very similar to Booth's apparently unconnected usage.[56]

On the specific implications of this perspective, however, Giddens's account diverges very significantly from Booth's position. Whereas Booth argues for recasting security in terms of 'emancipation', Giddens maintains that 'emancipatory politics' is being historically transcended by 'life politics'. The difference is that, 'while emancipatory politics is a politics of life chances, life politics is a politics of lifestyle.'[57] The politics of emancipation – which are still one axis of contemporary politics – revolve around social inequality, exploitation and oppression. Giddens argues that life politics are emerging as the dominant agenda because they reflect the more specific characteristics of late modern society: 'a politics of life decisions', reflecting the situation of individuals in high modernity. Formally, they are defined as politics which concern

> political issues which flow from processes of self-actualisation in post-traditional contexts, where globalising influences intrude deeply into the reflexive project of the self, and conversely where processes of self-realisation influence global strategies.[58]

Life politics, therefore, are politics of risk and security in a more fundamental sense even than emancipatory politics, since risk and security become uniquely pervasive in the late modern era.

Life politics are, of course, far more developed, and far greater choice is possible, in the prosperous West than in many poorer parts of the world, where emancipatory politics are more central. Clearly there is an ethnocentrist danger in Giddens's case, but he argues that even the poor in most parts of the world are increasingly incorporated, via mass media, into the culture of modernity, and are thus affected (albeit at a very different level) by the same tendencies which are developing in the West.

Life politics and emancipatory politics in fact intersect, Giddens acknowledges, with 'life-political' issues raising 'emancipatory' problems, and vice versa. He gives as an example the relationship between economic growth in the developing world and global environmental problems, and contends that 'a process of emancipation on the part of the world's poor could probably only be achieved if radical lifestyle changes were introduced in the developed countries.'[59]

Giddens's view of the role of social groups in politics thus departs from a traditional sociological view in that he sees social groups not just in terms of preformed social categories with a capacity for agency (for example, the classic Marxian view of class), but as constituted *through* political action (for example, around environmental and other 'life-political' issues). Social movements are seen, as they were in *The Nation-State and Violence*, as key collective actors around the main axes of modernity.[60] Politics, in life politics, is defined primarily in the broad sense of choice in action which affects the social order, although the secondary sense which relates to the nation-state is also recognized.[61]

In general, however, it is clear that, unlike in *The Nation-State and Violence*, where a nation-state-divided global order was the focus of attention, in these new books Giddens assumes a developing global society which transcends the nation-state. But this is not explicitly discussed and, as Giddens does not supply us with the connecitons, we shall have to make them ourselves.

## The sociology of international security

The most basic significance of Giddens's account is that it clearly establishes security as a general problem for individuals and groups in society. It provides a historical framework for analysing the changes in the nature of security problems between pre-modern and modern times. It also provides a general account of risk and security in modern society, with a set of categories to explain this (I have concentrated, in this exposition, on certain of these – for example, abstract systems – but the argument is richer than there has been space to convey).

The fact that Giddens's two recent works hardly mention the state, although limiting their more obvious relevance to international relations, is useful in underlining the point that it is highly possible to discuss security without doing so. Individual and collective human security do not depend overwhelmingly on the state and/or ethnic-national context, as Buzan and Waever tend to suggest. Security issues are faced at all levels of social life. The concept of security is a general concept of social science – rather like that of strategy, which is also seen as special to international relations, but has in fact a broad significance for the social sciences.[62]

Giddens's work is important to the current international debate in that it provides a broader argument, in a 'utopian realist' perspective similar to Booth's, which widens and underpins the case for moving away from the state level in discussing security. Giddens's conceptualization of social movements, and insistence on seeing social groups as consti-tuted though political action rather than being objectively preformed, helps to clarify the nature of the 'communities' to which Booth refers, and gives one sort of sociological answer to the questions raised above.

It is useful to ask what happens to Giddens's argument about risk and security if we 'bring the state back in'. First, states become one sort of specialized bureaucracy monitoring and attempting to regulate risk; in Booth's sense, they become (but not uniquely: only alongside other institutions) 'providers' of security to individuals and groups within society. Second, however, states and the state system become a very important (but again, not by any means the only) context in which risk is generated for individuals and human groups. In both these senses, states (and international relations in the sense of what goes on between them) are specific instances of the wider processes which Giddens outlines.

There is a third point, however, which has to do with the specific character of the nation-state. States are unique, notably in claiming to represent 'sovereignty' and the monopoly of legitimate violence. In the 'reflexive monitoring' which Giddens indicates characterizes abstract systems, states have a dominant role, even if parallel activities are undertaken by many non-state organizations. As Giddens's own earlier work suggests, the combination of territoriality and legitimacy gives states a pivotal role in what he calls the 'surveillance' cluster of institutions in modern societies.[63]

At the very moment, however, at which Giddens defined this world of nation-states, each a 'bordered power container' mobilizing 'outward-pointing violence' against other states, this view – uncomfortably close to international relations realism, as we have indicated – was rapidly starting to lose much of the validity which it previously had. States began to crumble under the many pressures which had accumulated on that level of organization. Statehood began to fracture, so that some of its attributes could be seen as attaching themselves to supra-state institutions, while others were claimed by sub-state collectivities, often in the name of a plethora of newly revived nationalisms. Sovereignty no longer resided uniquely in one set of institutions easily labelled as 'nation-states', but was increasingly shared above and below.

This turmoil at and around the state level can, of course, be incorporated, as it is by Buzan and Waever, in sophisticated versions of a relatively traditional state/nation-centred version of international relations. It can be interpreted more productively, however, as evidence of the interpenetration of state and other levels of society. The international system of relations between states can be seen as a system which increasingly constitutes what Giddens describes as an 'institutionalized risk environment', reflexively monitored by the 'players' (states) but also by others (individuals, social groups) influenced by its operations. This system is influenced by other such environments at a global level (for example, economic relations, monetary order, socially created ecological systems) as well as influencing them. It also interpenetrates with systems which exist within states.

Recent sociological work can thus assist in developing a more broadly conceived 'security studies', which in turn refocuses the questions of 'international security studies' with which we began this paper. Giddens's work has, however, as we have seen, its own limitations, from a sociological as well as an international relations point of view. We can conclude, therefore, that at the moment sociology is better placed to pose conceptual challenges to international studies than to give definitive answers. In moving beyond the statism/individualism dichotomy, we need to broaden the conceptual basis as well as the issue agenda of the study of security. In the process, we will also redefine the issues in sociological terms.

In arguing that society is the missing dimension of international security studies, this chapter has rejected the concept of *a* society as the basis for a sociological approach. It has argued instead that we need to understand the global flux of social relations within which the international system floats, and to explore the manifold dimensions of these relations. This conception suggests a new analytical agenda for a sociologically oriented international relations or a globally and internationally focused sociology. How far does a global society exist? What are the security concerns of individuals and groups within an emergent global society? Which sorts of groups are there and how do they articulate their concerns? What are the relationships between social movements, institutions and states? How do such concerns intersect with the international state system, and how far do concepts and policies of national and international security reflect such wider concerns within society? Related to this, of course, is a moral and political agenda: the answers to these questions will feed into concerns with the development of communities at local, national, regional and global levels, and contribute to a conception of community which is based not so much on an international community of states as on a global community of human beings.

## NOTES

1   Ken Booth, 'Security and emancipation', *Review of International Studies*, 17, 4, 1991, p. 317.
2   See, for example, the discussion in Owen Greene, 'Transnational processes and European security'. In M. Pugh, ed., *European Security: Towards 2000*, Manchester: Manchester University Press, 1992, pp. 141–61.
3   My discussion of Buzan, *People, States and Fear*, is based on the second edition, newly subtitled *An Agenda for International Security Studies in the Post-Cold War Era*, Hemel Hempstead: Harvester-Wheatsheaf, 1991.
4   Steve Smith, 'Mature anarchy, strong states and security' (review article on Buzan), in *Arms Control*, forthcoming.

5 Booth, p. 317.
6 Booth, p. 317.
7 Buzan, p. 1.
8 Buzan, p. 5.
9 Buzan, p. 13.
10 Buzan, p. 19.
11 Buzan, p. 70.
12 James Mayall, *Nationalism and International Society*, Cambridge: Cambridge University Press, 1990, pp. 2–3.
13 Buzan, p. 70.
14 Buzan mentions almost in passing that 'in modern usage a nation is defined as a large group of people sharing the same cultural, and possibly the same ethnic or racial, heritage' (p. 70). This loose formulation is hardly satisfactory.
15 Benedict Anderson, *Imagined Communities*, 2nd edn, London: Verso, 1991.
16 Buzan, p. 19.
17 Buzan, p. 26.
18 The inadequacy of such a view was indicated long ago in Marx's critique of 'political freedom' in his 'On the Jewish Question' (1844): see T. B. Bottomore, ed., *Karl Marx: Early Writings*, London: C. A. Watts, 1964, pp. 1–41. While I would not uphold Marx *in toto*, his discussion of the limitations of the view which considers individuals purely from the standpoint of their participation in the state is of general sociological significance. A current attempt to make this aspect of Marx's *oeuvre* effective in a critical account of international relations can be seen in work in progress by Justin Rosenberg.
19 Buzan, p. 44.
20 Buzan, p. 47.
21 Buzan, p. 54.
22 Buzan, p. 57.
23 Buzan, p. 59.
24 Buzan, pp. 59–60.
25 Buzan, p. 60.
26 Buzan, pp. 96–107. He describes it as 'a powerful modifier of the state-centric view' in a comment on an earlier version of this paper (reviewer's note).
27 Buzan, p. 98.
28 Buzan, pp. 62–3.
29 Smith, 'Mature anarchy, strong states and security'.

30  Booth, 'Security and emancipation', p. 320.

31  Booth, p. 321.

32  Booth, p. 321.

33  Max Weber, *The Philosophy of the Social Sciences*, Glencoe, IL: Free Press, 1949.

34  I am indebted on this point to the very interesting discussion of Paul A. Chilton, 'On the embedding of the term "security" in language and conceptual systems', paper to the British International Studies Association Conference, Warwick, 1991.

35  A most paradoxical feature of the debate in international studies is that, while denying 'society' in the more fundamental sense in which it is used by sociology, international relations theorists do use the term 'society' in an altogether different context, in the sense of 'international society'. This conception compounds the statism of international security studies which has been criticized above; a full discussion of it is given in Chapter 5.

36  Ken Booth, 'Security in anarchy: utopian realism in theory and practice', *International Affairs*, 67, 3, 1991, especially pp. 540–1 *et seq.*

37  Ole Wæver, 'Societal security: the concept'. In Wæver, Barry Buzan, Morten Kelstrup and Pierre Lemaitre, *Identity, Migration and the New Security Agenda in Europe*, London: Pinter, 1993, pp. 15–40.

38  Giddens, *The Nation-State and Violence*, p. 163, quoted in Wæver, p. 19.

39  Wæver, p. 19.

40  Wæver, p. 20.

41  R. B. J. Walker, 'Security, sovereignty and the challenge of world politics', *Alternatives*, XV, 1, p. 5, quoted in Wæver, p. 20.

42  Wæver, p. 21.

43  Wæver, p. 22.

44  Hakan Wiberg, 'Societal security and the explosion of Yugoslavia', in Wæver et al., *Identity, Migration and the New Security Agenda in Europe*, pp. 93–109.

45  So much so that, when we renamed our Centre for Defence and Disarmament Studies at Hull as a 'Centre for Security Studies' – omitting the specializing 'International' which Buzan gives his book – we found ourselves in some difficulty with the criminologists in our School!

46  Giddens, *The Consequences of Modernity*, Cambridge: Polity, 1990, p. 7.

47  Ibid., pp. 157–8.
48  Giddens, *Modernity and Self-Identity*, Cambridge: Polity, 1991, p. 4.
49  Ibid., pp. 35–88.
50  Ibid., pp. 111–12.
51  Ibid., pp. 115–16.
52  Ibid., p. 119.
53  Ibid., p. 121.
54  Ibid., p. 133.
55  Ibid., p. 136.
56  Giddens, *The Consequences of Modernity*, pp. 154–8; Booth, 'Security in anarchy', especially pp. 533–9.
57  Giddens, *Modernity and and Self-Identity*, p. 214.
58  Ibid., p. 214.
59  Ibid., p. 230.
60  Giddens, *The Nation-State and Violence*, and *The Consequences of Modernity*, pp. 158–63.
61  Giddens, *Modernity and Self-Identity*, pp. 226–7.
62  See Lawrence Freedman's contribution to Gerald Segal, ed., *New Directions in Strategic Studies*, London: RIIA, 1989, in which he argues for what I criticize (in the same symposium) as an 'imperialistic' view of strategic studies in relation to the social sciences. There is, however, a difference between 'strategy' and 'security' in that the former has specifically military origins – see my 'Strategy and social process: military context and sociological analysis', *Sociology*, 24, 3, 1990, pp. 465–73 – while the latter does not.
63  Giddens, *The Nation-State and Violence*.

*Five*

# The Limits of
# 'International Society'

The concept of society in general – society as opposed to the state – is, we have seen in Chapter 4, a structural absence in international relations theory. Where society is admitted, it is in the limited sense of *a* society, in which it is identified with nation and ethnic group, themselves the social concomitants of states. While this absence or narrowness of sociological perspective weakens international theory's understanding of the breadth and depth of security issues, as we argued above, it also greatly inhibits its understanding of global society. It leads international theorists to deny the existence or minimize the relevance of global society, and to give ontological priority to the international system, or the state system as we have called it in this book. The international system, we are led to believe, is a firm reality which structures world events, global society a nebulous concept with weak roots in reality.

The very concept of the international is, of course, highly problematic in the light of the discussion in the previous chapter. International refers, in reality, either to relations between states or, at a minimum, to relations across state boundaries which are significantly structured by those bound-aries. The concept of the international is inherently statist, and, although it is difficult to avoid using this terminology which is so embedded in popular, political and academic language, we must always be aware of its incipient statism. Relations between states cannot be assumed to be relations between nations, and social relations across state or national boundaries cannot be assumed to be international.

The discourse within international relations theory which most acutely embodies the contradictions of the discipline is that of international society. International society, as used in this context, is neither international nor a society, but refers to a particular trend towards 'society-like' features in the state system. In this chapter we pursue the critique of 'society' in international theory, and the contradictions of a theory of relations between states which neglects their context in global society, by unravelling the meaning and historic significance of the idea of international society.

## Ideological significance of 'international society'

In order to assess the idea of international society, we must understand that the fates of theoretical concepts in the social sciences are intertwined with the development of historical reality. Concepts which are developed in an attempt to understand, even predict, the changing world are necessarily subject to the frequently unpredictable twists and turns of history. Concepts with an apparent mission to explain action are also often both articulations of how actors actually understand their actions and intended as guides to how they might act in the future. Social-scientific concepts are a part of what they try to explain, and their relevance, validity and indeed success is conditional on the part they play.

Another way of putting this argument, which might have been more favoured in the recent past than it will be today, is to say that social-scientific concepts have an 'ideological' character. Such a presentation of the case will meet with misunderstandings, associated as it is with Marxist attempts to explain away the mainstream of Western social science.[1] It is not, however, necessary to adopt a Marxist stance in order to utilize the concept of 'ideology'. Nor is it necessary, even in the Marxist conception, to impute complete, let alone deliberate, falsehood to a theory because of its ideological character.

On the contrary, to suggest the ideological aspect of a theory is first of all to stress its historical *significance*. An ideology has a role in relation to the world of social action which a 'purely' academic theory would lack. An ideologically important theory will also be valid, at least in that it will express important truths and a major viewpoint of a historical period, and probably in that it will articulate more lasting knowledge in the context of its time. The implication of an ideological critique is, however, that the theory is limited by its time and viewpoint, and its aim is to explicate its contradictions so as to develop a more historically adequate theory. (Such an approach need not necessarily imply, as it would in a Marxist schema, a concept of historical progress; it is also compatible with a discontinuist concept of historical change, since it is the fact of change which is important rather than its content or sequence.)

The theory of international society[2] can be understood, it is argued here, as a central ideology of the international system in the Cold War period. This argument is presented not in order to deny the relevance of the theory, but to identify how the important insights into the system which it provides were connected to the nature of the period in which the theory was developed, and represented one position on it. Nor is this argument put forward to deny the continuing relevance of these same insights; it does, however, suggest that we have reached the moment of their maximum validity, that the contradictions of the perspective are now unfolding, and that its theoretical foundations can now be seen to be fundamentally lacking.

The argument may seem paradoxical in that, at first glance, the international society perspective does indeed seem to have gained a coherence in the post-Cold War era which it previously lacked; indeed, as we shall see, a central weakness of the case has been removed by the end of the Cold War. It is at the moment of its greatest success that we can see the decisive importance of its contradictions and the need to move beyond the limited theoretical foundations which it provides.

## The crisis of 'international society' thinking

The concept of international society has been put forward by its advocates as a 'central' position for international studies, a modal alternative to the extremes of brutish Hobbesian realism and utopian Kantian idealism.[3] It incorporates the dominant realism of the subject, in its recognition of the dominance of independent sovereign states as actors in the international system; yet it makes a nod to idealism (as well as to social-scientific functionalism) in the role it assigns to consensus among actors as the basis for 'society'-like elements in the way this system develops. (This theoretical balancing act is a source of tensions in the theory, as Nicholas Wheeler shows.)[4]

The international society position has, of course, its own (Grotian) philosophical antecedents; but it is essentially a modern theory, a product (like most of the discipline of international relations) of the unique international situation of the third quarter of the twentieth century. On first approach, the context of a bipolar conflict between rigidly ideologically opposed powers is hardly the most apposite one for a stance which stresses a consensual framework of relations between states. However, Hedley Bull argued that, even in the depths of the Cold War, the idea of international society 'survived as an important part of reality'.[5]

It is perhaps the major achievement of writers such as Bull, and the great strength of the largely British-based international society school, to have recognized the elements of cooperation which underlay the apparently irreconcilable Cold War opposition. Much more than the school of strategically oriented international relations, dominant in the United States, which stressed technological rivalry, it has been vindicated by the outcome of the Cold War. To a greater extent than even Bull seems to have thought likely, a shared set of expectations and understandings dominated the behaviour of the political elites in the USA and former USSR. This led – after the crisis of the 'Second Cold War' – to a relatively orderly unwinding (at the level of superpower relations at least) of the Cold War.

That the international society perspective stressed the framework of common understandings among states (despite the unpromising Cold War context) is testimony to the strength of broader historical understanding which it brought to the study of the international system. Bull, Wight[6] and others were able to see the Cold War system in the context of a longer historical development and to ask many of the right comparative questions, pointing to the strengths as well as the weaknesses of contemporary international society while taking into account past models.

It might be thought perverse, in this light, to see the international society position as framed by the Cold War era. Insofar as it has political implications, it was clearly never a Cold Warrior stance in the narrow partisan sense. While its emphasis on the possibilities of the balance of power might have pointed to the long-term maintenance of the Cold War system, it also opened possibilities of a critical interpretation which promised to transcend the Cold War. For so long as entrenched Cold War hostilities rendered the society element uncertain, there was a strong argument to be made for moving beyond this to a more stable basis of international society.

The case for seeing the international society approach as an ideology of the Cold War period – at its best a historically sophisticated and potentially critical ideology with much to offer to any understanding of the international system – lies elsewhere. Essentially it is found in a weakness which is common to virtually all schools of international relations, as the discipline has developed in the 'post-war' period. Like most international relations literature, the writings of the international society school operate with a fundamentally state-centric approach. They are concerned with the international system first and foremost – Bull presents society as an element in that system – and with other realities only as they impinge on that system. Thus although Bull presents world society and world politics as logically and morally prior to international society, he presents no coherent perspective on these which informs his account of the international. Indeed, writing in 1977, he regarded world society as at best an emergent reality.[7]

It might be thought obvious that the international system forms a relatively discrete order of reality, distinct from even as it interacts with world politics in a wider sense, and more broadly with world economy, culture and society. Certainly, modern states behave as though this is the case in most of their dealings with one another which make up the international system; and empirically it seems correct to describe the development of the framework of self-regulation among modern states, which is called international society. This self-evident separateness of the international system, and within it of international society, is, however, something which needs to be explained and critically examined.

Just as discussions of international society have their favourite historical periods, such as that of the early nineteenth-century Concert of Europe, they have their rather noticeable absences. It is rather difficult, as even Bull himself acknowledges, to see Hitler's Germany and Stalin's Russia as bound by common norms of international society. What such questions raise is the issue of whether the Cold War period was itself special in any way – apart from the bipolarization and ideologization of international conflict already mentioned, or its nuclearization which obviously had specific effects – which is pertinent to the theory.

The case which can be made is that the Cold War was unique in the twentieth century in the predominance of international relations over domestic politics and society. The first half of the century saw a dialectic of national and international politics in which neither could be said to be simply dominant. The First World War first subsumed deep the social tensions and political divides in the industrial societies which had developed in the nineteenth century; it then regenerated these in the revolutionary and counter-revolutionary movements of the inter-war years; these movements (notably Fascism and communism) in turn fed into international tensions, polarizing Europe and the world between ideologically polarized states.[8]

The Second World War destroyed Fascism and turned Stalinism into a ruling ideology in the East but a domesticated oppositional form of labour politics in the West. Its outcome left the single ideologized confrontation between the Soviet Union and the West dominating the politics of all states in the northern hemisphere. Uniquely in modern history outside war situations, the international unequivocally dominated society and domestic politics. The bipolar conflict largely neutralized – even froze – many minor international conflicts, but it also froze national politics into Cold War variants (Christian democracy, social democracy, Stalinism), and had many corresponding effects in society and culture.

It was in this atypical predominance of international over national politics, with a corresponding reduction of the influence of politics in the wider sense over the international, that international relations grew as a discipline. Theories such as that of international society emphasized the coherence of relations among states as distinct from other political and social relations. (In this context, too, as we saw in Chapter 2, sociologists who turned their attention to these issues emphasized the completeness of nation-states' 'surveillance' of societies and the 'geopolitical privacy of states' in relation to their populations.)[9]

All this is now history (as the saying goes). The Cold War period itself contained, as we saw in Chapter 3, major prefigurations of the re-emergence of national revolt and social protest as factors in international politics – the revolts of Eastern European peoples, from Berlin in 1953 to Gdansk in 1980, and the peace movements in Western Europe in the early 1980s. All of these were, in their time, defeated, and hence could be seen as ultimately unimportant to the East–West conflict. The crisis of 1989, however, involved a dialectic of superpower detente and Soviet reform with the mass democratic movements in East Germany and Czechoslovakia, which ushered in the most fundamental change in the international system since 1945.[10]

The years since 1989 have seen an escalation of the role of sub-international politics in the international system. Nationalist and ethnic politics in the parts of the former Soviet Union and Eastern Europe have led to an instability of the state system in Europe not seen since the 1940s, with wars in ex-Yugoslavia (threatening a general Balkan war), and between Armenia and Azerbaijan, and in Moldova and Georgia (all of which threaten to involve Russia and a range of other states, both ex-Soviet republics and others). The dialectic of political movements and international relations, so apparently virtuous in 1989, has become much more vicious in its aftermath. The revival of nationalism may be seen, following Mayall's discussion, as a normal part of the renewal of international society[11] – even Bosnian Serbs seek a place in the community of states for their ethnic mini-state, suitably 'cleansed' of their former neighbours – but it also raises issues of the *extent* to which sub-national developments dictate the international agenda.

As EU and UN mediators scurry after the minor ethnic warlords of the fragments of Bosnia, Croatia and other ex-Yugoslav republics, as UN troops wobble uncertainly between peacekeeping and peacemaking, as the great powers trade the dangers of intervention against the dangers of a public outcry at (mass mediated) civilian misery and death, it is obvious that something has changed. 'Turbulence in world politics' is not new, but its intensity has been increasing, and in the post-Cold War era is breaking up the insulated categories of international theory in a way which fulfils Rosenau's prophetic view of 'post-international' politics.[12]

In this situation, international society seems *both* more surely founded and more problematic. The proponents of the concept can take heart from the removal of the Cold War ideological fracture which centrally threatened the cultural coherence of a 'society'. It is now manifest that the major players are the Western powers among whom the rules and underlying assumptions are widely shared; Russia and other ex-communist states are eager to vow allegiance to the same norms and institutions.

It is possible, as Buzan has argued, to see emerging a gigantic northern 'security community'.[13] This could stretch from North America and Western Europe to the major states of the former USSR and Eastern Europe, and to Japan, the newly industrializing states of East Asia, and Australasia. China, as a regional great power and permanent member of the Security Council, is partially implicated, although its democratization would consolidate its membership and underline the growing implicit connection between international society and political democracy. Other powers, from India, to Egypt, to Brazil, to (a reformed) South Africa, may equally be involved in regional extensions of this community.

At the very moment, however, when such developments seem to strengthen what is referred to as international society, other changes bring it into question.[14] Increasingly it is the interactions between the international system and wider social and political changes which command our attention. International relations between states are to an increasing extent *about* issues within societies, as the crises of 1991–2 have shown. The Anglo-French-American intervention in northern Iraq was a direct response to media-political pressure in Western societies resulting from the plight of the Kurdish people, even if this was an indirect consequence of the war in Iraq. The Western powers' intervention, increasingly under UN auspices, in Bosnia has progressively been under the impetus of humanitarian concerns resulting from similarly mediated pressure, even if there are more traditional international issues at stake.[15]

These changes are increasingly modifying what have been seen as the assumptions and institutions of international society. The principles of sovereignty and non-intervention are more and more problematic. The assumption that international policing is a matter for the great powers, while still holding a good deal of force, is nevertheless qualified by the enlarged role of the UN in coordinating as well as legitimating intervention. No doubt it will be argued that in none of these respects has anything fundamental changed, but this is to ignore the corrosive effects of the *ad hoc* modifications to international practice, now occurring at a rapid rate. All these changes raise the question of the adequacy of the *theoretical* perspective of international society.

## International society and global society

The concept of international society is seen by its proponents alongside that of international system. The concept of system is the more fundamental and less problematic: it simply requires us to recognize patterns of interactions between states as possessing a coherence which, at least in part, determines their actions and possibly those of others. Bull, whose account of the relationship of system and society is the most careful, recognizes the nebulous character of international society by proclaiming it no more than an 'element' in the international system.[16] At the same time, however, he very definitely writes as though it has a capacity for action, as when it acts in common to assure its goals, which seems to ascribe to it a greater degree of reality than that of a mere element in a system.

The concept of an international society is unusual, in a way that that of a system is not, in that societies are usually defined in terms of social relations among individual human beings. International relations as a discipline has the general problem, as we argued in Chapter 4, in its state-centredness, treatment of states as actors akin to individuals, and neglect of the complex social relations which bind individuals and states. Bull recognizes this in a discussion, rather curious to the sociological eye, of the similarities and differences between the self-regulating society of states (lacking a central political authority) and the primitive stateless societies described by anthropologists.[17] Formally, such a comparison may be quite possible, but Bull ignores the substantive difficulties which arise when we discuss a society composed of what are 'already' (that is, as a result of 'domestic' characteristics not considered by international theorists) social institutions.

What is apparent here is that the concept and terminology of international society only work providing that the insulation of international studies from theoretical discourse with other social sciences is maintained. Such an insulation cannot be justified in the name of a division of labour in the social sciences. Certainly there is a case that states are very distinctive and important kinds of social institutions, the interactions among which are equally distinctive, and in this sense require a specific mode of understanding which implies a discipline. There is no case to can be sustained, however, which denies the common features between the state and other social institutions or the connections between state–civil society and state–state relations, in the general context of world society. In this sense international relations must be theoretically integrated with the mainstream of the social sciences. Its concepts should be developed not just by analogy with other social sciences – as in Bull's discussion of a stateless society – but consistently with them. The substantive connections between the concepts of international relations and of other social sciences must be clear.

Bull's discussion of international society lays bare a crucial problem in the way he gives a particular meaning to society. By defining society in terms of a consensus between its members he gives a great deal of weight to its normative coherence. There are, of course, approaches in sociology and anthropology, normally described as functionalist, which have adopted precisely such an approach – although Bull hardly acknowledges the connection.[18] These approaches are widely discredited, however, not just because they tended to underrate social conflict, but because they define society in terms of one of its dimensions – with reference to the discussion in Chapter 1, of social rather than system integration. Precisely the same could be said of Bull.

As we argued in that chapter, human society can be defined by the existence of relationships involving mutual expectations and understandings, with the possibility of mutually oriented actions. In this sense, society can be said to be far more akin, formally, to the meaning of system used in international relations; the concept of society does not, except in the systems of thought constructed by some functionalists, require consensus around coherent value systems. The existence of such systems is an empirical question, among many others which arise in analysing societies.

From this discussion we can see that, even from a formal point of view, the distinction between system and society is suspect. Even if it were not – if we could accept the identification of society and consensus – there is still the question of the substantive (and terminological) relationship between international society and human society or societies in a wider sense. The terminological issue is not the most important, but it bears thinking about, since it is potentially confusing to talk of a society of states when most societies are understood to be composed of individual human beings. The substantive issue is more important: is international 'society' a sub-set of some kind (a sub-culture?) of human society in some wider sense? Or is it self-sufficient, with no theoretically articulable relationship to the larger pattern of human relations?

Reading Bull, we are left with the feeling that the relationship by analogy may be as important as any substantive relationship. World society is acknowledged as a reference point, and together with world politics is accorded notional priority over the international. World society is, however, seen as something which at best is just starting to come into existence; it does not exist in the way in which international society does. We see, therefore, that the priority of world society is purely nominal, since in any sense which counts the society of states is quite obviously stonger, indeed has greater reality. But this conception of world society betrays the same strong meaning of society which we noted above: world society does not exist, for Bull, because it lacks the coherent, shared values and framework of understanding which, to a degree at least, international society possesses.

What if world society or, in today's parlance, global society does exist? In the weaker sense of a global system of social relations, in which all human beings are to some extent connected, and which covers the entire globe, we do indeed have such a world society. Indeed, whereas in the past it might have made sense to talk of discrete human societies, today the concept of 'a society' can only be applied fully and consistently, as we argued in Chapter 1, to human society on a world scale. Other usages, whether referring to national, ethnic or tribal societies (British, Kurdish, Zulu) are increasingly arbitrary abstractions from the global flux of social relations.[19] World society exists through the social relations involved in global commodity production and exchange, through global culture and mass media, and through the increasing development of world politics.

The international system of states may appear to be one of the most important, or at least the most developed, systems which order global society; but it is not the only set of institutions to be increasingly organized on a global scale, for economic and cultural institutional networks have global reach as well, and we can also talk about these as powerful systems within global society. It may even be the case that we can begin to talk about global society in terms of the development of common values and beliefs and a common political culture, in which ideas of democracy and national status, for example, are widely diffused.

How are the concepts of global society and international society to be related? It is difficult to explore this issue clearly starting from the concepts supplied by Bull and his co-thinkers. First of all, if global society is defined in terms of a weak (social relationships) and international society in terms of a strong (common values, consensus) meaning of society, the relationship is logically complex. Secondly, there is a case for distinguishing between a society of human individuals and one of states. Thirdly, it is highly desirable that our conceptualization should assist in defining the transformation of relationships between the international and the global. At the very least, there is a case for a terminological adjustment, but this would seem merely to be an entailment of a substantive theoretical reformulation.

It is proposed here, following from the discussion in Chapter 1, that we should distinguish between a society, its culture and institutions. Social relationships on a world scale constitute a society (weak sense). Within this global society, there is a global economic system, with not only world markets, but globally coordinated production. There are increasingly the elements of a global culture, including a political culture, but there are also very many segmentations corresponding to state, national, ethnic, religious, political, class, cultural and lifestyle divisions. Within this global society, too, there are numerous global institutions, among which the state system (international system) is pre-eminent but not exclusively dominant, as well as many more locally based institutions.

From the point of view of global society, the development of what is called international society is *the development of the institutions and the institutional culture of the state system* in the direction of greater coherence and consensus. Redefining international society in this way, we look at it as a development specific to the state system, but one which reflects this system's role in global society. It is the product not only of developments within the system, but also of the system's articulation with the structures, culture and other institutions of that society.

Viewed in this theoretical light, the development of what is called international society can no longer be seen in purely contingent relationship to the development of global society. Certainly there is no automatic, mechanical connection between globalization (in the sense of the extension and increasing integration of global society) and the integration of the state system, seen in terms of international society. The latter has its own dynamics which do indeed need to be investigated empirically, both in themselves and in terms of their many and complex relationships with other manifestations of globalization. Developments in the state system must, however, be studied in the context of the entire picture of the development of world society, which does indeed have theoretical priority.

Adopting this standpoint, we need an understanding of the way in which the processes of economic expansion and cultural diffusion have increasingly created an integrated world society – of which a more tightly integrated state system is an inevitable part. The problem is that global economic integration has been studied apart from the development of the state system, and global cultural integration has hardly been studied at all in general terms. These three main sets of processes are, however, what have together (over centuries and especially the last few decades) created the basis of a world society.

This perspective is important to current international relations debates because it explains *why* the international system is increasingly not self-sufficient; why sub- and supra-national actors are of growing importance in international politics; why, indeed, we are looking at post-international politics. It explains why we should stop seeing non-state actors as intruders into the system and society of states, and see them instead as actors within global society of which the state system is an institutional component, and whose intrusion is therefore entirely normal and inevitable. It explains why the moral priority which Bull rightly accorded in principle to world society and politics over international society is not of purely utopian significance (as he seemed to believe) but of the utmost practical import in dealing with the issues of the day.

## From the ideology of states to global responsibility

The Cold War situation, in which the international state system contained the emergence of global society, is coming to an end. Groups, movements and institutions within global society are making themselves felt within the international state system which politically mediates global social relations. It is only right and proper that they should do so, even if it threatens the assumptions of the state system and challenges the norms of international society such as sovereignty and non-intervention. This is not to say that these norms are wholly redundant, but is to insist that they must be qualified by general accountability to the needs and wishes of the members of global society.

We should welcome this process, however embryonic it may

be, and however many strains it introduces into the state system which will then spill over into the lives of people within global society. What is involved, however modestly and contradictorily, is the beginning of the development of what we may call *global civil society*, in which members of global society are starting to try to make the state system responsible – in the way in which national civil societies have, in the past, generated pressures to ensure the accountability of national states.

At the core of the development of global civil society is the concept of *global responsibility*. Again embryonically, this idea can be seen at work in a variety of developments – the attempts by global ecological movements to make the state system respond to demands for global environmental management; the attempts by pressure groups to ensure that human rights and democracy are judged by a global standard; and the demands, fuelled by media coverage, to make respect for human needs and human rights effective principles in international conflicts. The pressure on Western governments to intervene to protect the Kurds – to accept responsibility for the indirect victims of their war against Iraq – and to intervene for purely humanitarian reasons in Bosnia-Herzogovina are very recent manifestations of this principle of global responsibility.

Each of these recent interventions has implicitly or explicitly challenged the principles of sovereignty and non-intervention which have been seen as core assumptions of international society. The principles have, of course, been waived or varied in response to similar pressures in the past, and there is nothing to suggest that states are yet willing to subordinate them largely, yet alone entirely, to principles of global responsibility. Rather there has been a real struggle between the instincts of statesmen to maintain the principles of sovereignty and non-intervention, and the pressure from global civil society to transcend them.

The instincts of President Bush and Mr Major were to abstain, in practical terms, from the civil conflicts in Iraq after the Gulf War, even after they had morally and politically incited rebellion against Saddam Hussein. The Shi'as of southern Iraq were effectively abandoned to their fate in March 1991 with US troops a matter of miles from Basra, the main centre of rebellion. The Kurds were likewise abandoned until international political and media pressure suddenly built up in mid-April 1991. Even after intervention, the allies and the UN maintained the fiction of Iraqi sovereignty in seeking Iraqi agreement to the operation of UN relief agencies (the fiction cost them dearly in official currency rates and other Iraqi rake-offs). Nevertheless, in military terms the ceasefire agreement itself breached Iraqi sovereignty by providing for intensive UN surveillance of Iraqi military preparations.

In this episode, it was quite clear that Western leaders were operating with an ideology of international society, in which the defeated Iraqi state, however exposed as morally and politically bankrupt, was still accorded the rights and prerogatives of a sovereign state. While the allies were prepared to breach these in their own state interests (the control of weapons of mass destruction) they still upheld the concept of non-intervention where it was merely an issue of a threat to Iraq's own citizens. Only under severe political pressure from an implicit stance of global responsibility did they concede intervention.

In the Yugoslav case, the ideology of international society operated against any idea of intervention when it first became apparent – in the repression of Kosovo in the later 1980s – that an aggressive nationalist regime had come to power in Serbia which was precipitating the break-up of Yugoslavia. The conception that these were the domestic problems of a sovereign state prevailed, as Western states and international bodies continued to recognize Yugoslavia long after its demise had become inevitable, and without seriously attempting to intervene to regulate the break-up in terms of principles such as respect for existing borders, the rights of minorities and human rights in general. When the bankruptcy of this policy was finally apparent, the EC transferred its recognition to the new states of Slovenia and Croatia (but not Macedonia), again without attempting to regulate the conditions for Croatian independence in a way which would have created an acceptable recognition of Serbian minority rights. Its actions only stimulated the war in Croatia, which it then ineffectually attempted to monitor, and paved the way for the war in Bosnia-Herzegovina.

In the final irony, although recognizing the new Bosnian state and notionally admitting it to international society, the West made no attempt to help secure its reality on the ground but largely abandoned it to its fate. Only when the media made it clear that this potentially included the slow starvation of half a million people in Sarajevo, the 'ethnic cleansing' of over a million Muslims and Croats, massacres and concentration camps, did the pressure of global civil society push the West to define – at the London conference of August 1992 – the principles with which it should have tried to regulate the situation, politically, from 1989 or 1990 onwards, so as to prevent war. Under this pressure, too, Western European military intervention increased under UN auspices but without any clear political goals. By mid-1993 it was evident that Western states were unwilling seriously to defend threatened civilians in this crisis.

The international society ideology of Western states has been cruelly exposed in these crises. On an *as hoc* basis, forces from within the emerging global civil society have proposed different principles of intervention. What is surely required now is to systematize the demands of global responsibility in a new conception of the roles, rights and duties of citizens, society, states, the system of states and international institutions. Much of the intellectual infrastructure for such a conception is already available in the principles previously adopted by international organizations and theoretically subscribed to by states, as well as in the positions adopted by groupings in civil society. The crucial issue, then, is to face up to the necessity which enforcing these principles would impose to breach systematically the principles of sovereignty and non-intervention. A global society perspective requires recognition in the institutions and culture of the state system of the demands of society for accountability. This must include the increasingly systematic intervention of international society and international institutions in individual states which fail to meet acceptable standards.

This process, moreover, is not merely a matter of disciplining an Iraq or a Serbia, but involves issues such as the role of the USA, Japan and the European Union states in the distribution of global wealth and the use of energy resources; it could also involve calling the USA to account for unilateral military interventions like those in Grenada and Panama. In this sense, the issues raised are large and the interests threatened are to some extent those of all states. This means, of course, that we are unlikely to see a fundamental and explicit shift in the direction advocated here. The issues are likely to remain foci of contestation over a very long period of time.

The global society perspective, therefore, has an ideological significance which is ultimately opposed to that of international society. No decisive result can be expected, at a political and ideological level, to the conflict between these two positions, for the simple reason that, while the pressures for global responsibility are growing, the strength of the international system and of the great powers within it are still formidable.[20] While the global society perspective can no longer be dismissed, as Bull dismissed Falk's earlier raising of global environmental perspectives, as naive or utopian,[21] it is unlikely to become central to world politics in the short or medium term. What can be done is for international theorists and theorists of global society to clarify the relations between different systems of concepts, with the aim of producing consistent ideas which clarify the new realities of the post-Cold War era. It is to this task that this chapter has addressed itself, in the hopes of pointing out the ideological character and theoretical, historical and political limitations of the international society perspective.

## NOTES

1  The present writer made such an attempt in *Marxism and Social Science: The Roots of Social Knowledge*, London: Pluto, 1975;

for an auto-critique, see the introduction to my edited work *Marxist Sociology Revisited*, London: Macmillan, 1985.

2 The term international society and similar theoretical terms are used throughout this chapter without quotation marks. This is not because the author believes that they exist, or that they are appropriate theoretical concepts with which to describe or explain reality, but simply because to use quotation marks would make the text extremely messy. The chapter is about the appropriateness of international society and similar concepts, and the author's views on which of these concepts should be employed will be made clear in due course.

3 Hedley Bull, *The Anarchical Society*, London: Macmillan, 1977, pp. 25 –7. Bull's modern classic is referred to here as a representative work.

4 Nicholas J. Wheeler, 'Pluralist or solidarist conceptions of international society: Bull and Vincent on humanitarian intervention', *Millenium*, 21, 3, 1992, pp. 463–88. The reader is referred to this paper for a fuller exposition of Bull's version of 'international society' theory. I have benefited considerably from Wheeler's discussion, although, as will be seen, there are fundamental differences between our approaches.

5 Bull, p. 43.

6 Martin Wight, *Systems of States*, Leicester: Leicester University Press, 1977.

7 'The world society or community whose common good they [theorists of world justice] purport to define does not exist except as an idea or myth which may one day become powerful, but has not done so yet.' Bull, p. 85.

8 I have discussed these processes in my *Dialectics of War: An Essay on the Social Theory of War and Peace*, London: Pluto, 1988.

9 Anthony Giddens, *The Nation-State and Violence*, Cambridge: Polity, 1985, and Michael Mann, *States, War and Capitalism*, Oxford: Blackwell, 1988.

10 I have discussed this more fully in 'State theory and the post-Cold War world'. In Micheal Banks and Martin Shaw, eds, *State and Society in International Relations*, Hemel Hempstead: Harvester-Wheatsheaf, 1991, pp. 1–19.

11 James Mayall, *Nationalism and International Society*, Cambridge: Cambridge University Press, 1990.

12  James N. Rosenau, *Turbulence in World Politics*, Hemel Hempstead: Harvester-Wheatsheaf, 1990.

13  Barry Buzan, 'New patterns of global security in the twenty-first century', *International Affairs*, 67, 3, 1991, pp. 436–7. Buzan limits this community to the major capitalist powers, but the extensions I discuss seem reasonable developments of this argument.

14  The strengthening of international society is cautiously claimed by Buzan, pp. 437–9, while reiterating that 'the foundation of modern international society is the mutual recognition by states of each each other's claim to sovereignty.' This is, however, precisely what is brought into question by recent developments.

15  The breaches of the principles of sovereignty and non-intervention in the Kurdish case are explained away by James Mayall in terms of an international obligation arising 'because the coalition had inflicted such damage on Iraq as to reduce the country to chaos, making rebellion all but inevitable.' He argues therefore that 'it would be imprudent in practice, and wrong in theory, to generalise from the international obligations towards the Kurds in favour of an international enforcement mechanism for human rights wherever they are abused. . . . the obligation towards the Kurds does not arise from a general principle of human solidarity.' ('Non-intervention, self-determination and the "new world order" ', *International Affairs*, 67, 3, 1991, pp. 427–8. This argument does not, however, deal with the Bosnian case, in which 'a general principle of human solidarity' has indeed been invoked, albeit to limited effect.

16  Bull, p. 41.

17  Bull, pp. 59–65.

18  Indeed, Bull dissociates himself from functionalism, pp. 75–6.

19  A telling discussion of this from an international relations point of view, which goes from the question 'Is Britain still Britain?' to 'Can there still be a "British" foreign policy?' is provided by William Wallace, 'British foreign policy after the Cold War', *International Affairs*, 68, 1, 1992, especially pp. 432–42.

20  It is still true, as Bull wrote, that 'the framework of international order is quite inhospitable to projects for the realisation of cosmopolitan or world justice', and almost as inhospitable to those for human justice (pp. 87–8). It is also true, however, that the issues which these terms represent have become stronger and

more pressing in the fifteen years since Bull's book was published, and notably since the end of the Cold War.

21  Bull, pp. 302–5; most of his criticisms of Falk hit home, but there is no need for a global society perspective to entail most of the points which are undermined.

# PART FOUR

# A New Global Politics

## Six

# The New Politics of War

The theoretical debates explored in this book have their corollaries in a new ferment – and indeed confusion – about appropriate political responses. In the final two chapters, the politics of the new international situation are explored in the light of the global society perspective. The wars of the post-Cold War era are posing classic issues of the legitimacy of armed violence – on the part of states, political movements and also international institutions – in new forms. They also pose issues of agency and strategy, especially within civil society, which challenge the conceptions of social movements during the previous period.

In this section of the book we approach the political implications of the new context from two angles. In this chapter we examine the ways in which socialist, and especially Marxist, concepts of war, which have been influential on the Western left, are fundamentally challenged by the new situation. It is argued that the redundancy of war between the major powers, combined with the resurgence of bloody conflicts on the margins of the Western world, creates a particularly acute dilemma to which the old positions of the left do not provide a valid response. There is an urgency to re-evaluate the legacy of the Cold War, and to build on the inter-state cooperation which has been established, rather than to condemn it in terms of traditional concepts of imperialism.

In Chapter 7, we extend this argument into a full-blown case for a politics of global responsibility, and examine the critical issues of the relationships between the institutions and means of state power, on the one hand, and the development of global civil society, on the other.

## The left and the politics of war

The political left throughout the world has yet to come to terms with the consequences of the end of the Cold War. The international system is undergoing fundamental change, but socialists are divided, not only among themselves but often within themselves, over how to respond to the change. The confused response to the challenge of the Gulf War represented the larger difficulties of the left in dealing with the new international situation. There is a crisis of socialist theory and practice which reflects the historic difficulties of the left in dealing with the issues raised by war and the international system. This section tries to outline the theoretical and political context which frames the current dilemmas.

The problem of war is a central one for any political position in any period. The politics of war can be framed in absolute terms of right and wrong, but these are rarely found adequate by large numbers of people. The nature of wars and the issues they pose are transformed in each historical period. This means that to transpose theories and political responses developed to deal with the wars of one period into a radically different succeeding stage is fraught with difficulties.[1]

Socialist thought has been particularly handicapped by weakly developed ideas of war and, throughout the twentieth century, by the persistence of attitudes to war inherited from its founders in the nineteenth. Classical socialist thought was formulated during the long nineteenth century 'peace' – the century between the end of the Napoleonic Wars in 1815 and the outbreak of the Great War in 1914. During this period, it was self-evident to most social theorists that the historic changes were those in economic organization and class structure rather than in warfare. Although the founders of Marxism never indulged themselves in the optimistic view of a peaceful industrial society which was advanced by Comte, and Engels is rightly celebrated as a military theorist, war hardly occupied a significant place in Marx's theoretical system. Changes in warfare were seen as consequences of the social and, above all, technological revolutions brought about by capitalist industrialization. They were not perceived as causes of major social, economic or political change.

The political corollary of this approach was a resolutely realist attitude towards war. For Marx and Engels, the major wars of their time (such as the American civil war) were important in so far as the victory of one side or the other advanced or hindered social and political progress. The later Engels saw some of the revolutionary potential of the contradictions in mass militarism, but neither he nor Marx viewed war as such as a political problem, any more than they saw it as a core theoretical issue. Their contempt for the ('petit bourgeois') pacifism which influenced more utopian strands of socialist thought reflected a consistent belief that the nature of war itself – as opposed to its consequences – was not a central issue.

These attitudes were reflected in Marx and Engels's response to Clausewitz, whose theory of war, derived from the Revolutionary and Napoleonic wars, can be seen in retrospect as a contribution to be compared with their own theorization of the socio-economic changes involved in the industrial revolution, and of the political changes involved in the French Revolution itself. The founding fathers of Marxism took from Clausewitz his analogy of warfare with commerce, and his insistence that war should be seen as a continuation of politics. They neglected his more fundamental insights on the nature of war: its special destructive character as a process based on force, its peculiarity as a very different means of continuing political struggle, its tendency towards 'absolute war'.

These characteristics of Marx and Engels's approach to war were carried over with disastrous results into the early twentieth-century heyday of revolutionary Marxism. Writers such as Luxemburg, Lenin and Bukharin, theorists of the age of imperialism, developed – with varying success – new theoretical models to explain the relationships of the economic, political and military dimensions of international competition. They did little, however, to pinpoint the ways in which the social organization of modern industrial capitalism – the creation of concentrated, disciplined workforces, and of mass politics and means of communication – had laid the foundation for a new mode of warfare, total war. Still less did they understand the social and political consequences of this form of warfare.

Even faced with the slaughter of the trenches, the response of revolutionary Marxists was resolutely within the realist frame bequeathed by the founders. Opposition to imperialist war was not opposition to war as such, but the basis for revolutionary civil war. There were those, like Luxemburg, whose appeals for resistance resonated with genuine anguish over the nature of the violence being perpetrated, and in whose hands the call for civil war seemed to lose its violent content and become almost purely political. The outcome, however, was hardly consonant with her humanitarianism: the civil war in Russia, on both sides, was as brutal as civil war can be.

The most important result of the failures of nineteenth-century socialists (especially Marxists) to theorize war and respond politically to war as a problem in its own right was that the fate of socialism became tied to war in ways which had not been foreseen, and which deformed the whole socialist project.[2]

Nineteenth-century socialists had agreed, to a very large extent, that socialism would involve the cooperative control of the associated producers over the means of production. They had agreed, to a similar degree, that the state would be less rather than more powerful – in Marx's phrase, notorious in the light of twentieth-century history, that it would wither away. As socialists began to see a prospect of power within parliamentary democracy they sought an accommodation with capitalism, and to use existing states for their own purposes. This turn towards statism among socialists reflected, however, the growing power of states in national economies and societies as war-preparation grew. The incorporation of the workers into parliamentary democracy was itself largely a trade-off for universal military service. The new citizenship of the mass bourgeois democracies equated political rights with military duty. Socialists still toyed with the more genuinely democratic idea of citizens' or workers' militias, but these were being overtaken by the statist direction of modern capitalism.

The statist trend in socialism was overwhelmingly confirmed by the actual experience of total war. State intervention produced war economies in most of the combatant states of 1914–18. In these economies, states planned, directed and even nationalized capital – and labour. They were described by many as 'war socialism', and although socialists saw that economies and states were still capitalist, many identified state intervention as a powerful demonstration of the possibilities of public action. The indigenous socialist traditions of Western countries became ever more fully statist, in a relatively benign reformist sense.

A similar fate overtook, with far greater vengeance, the revolutionary Marxism which succeeded in Russia. Civil war proved no mere extension of political struggle: in its harsh conditions the proletariat was decimated, the democracy of workers' councils became a sham, and the revolutionary party a near-monolith. The council-state became a party-state, and extreme centralism and dictatorship prospered. The Bolsheviks' lack of steer on war and militarism led some of their most talented thinkers to embrace the military commandism of 'war communism' as a model of the future – making a monstrous virtue out of appalling necessity. They were, it is evident with hindsight, literally digging their own graves, as the foundations were laid for Stalinist totalitarianism.[3]

As a result of war – world war, civil war – socialism in both its social-democratic and revolutionary forms had become irredeemably linked with statism. It could be said, of course, that for a whole historical period 'socialism' prospered in this association. The polarization of Europe between revolutionary communism, counter-revolutionary Fascism and parliamentary democracy, which resulted from the First World War, in turn led to a new, highly politicized and ideologized military conflict. In the aftermath of the Second World War, statism was a dominant trend in the Western world, and social democracy (in Western Europe at least) a major beneficiary. In Russia, Stalinism gained a new legitimacy from the patriotic struggle, while its armies annexed East-Central Europe to the 'socialist world', and militarized revolutions brought China, Yugoslavia and Albania, North Vietnam and North Korea into the 'socialist camp'.

We know now, of course, that this statization and militarization of socialism, in both its forms, was not only a distortion of the socialist project, but in the longer term self-defeating. The heyday of the welfare state in Western Europe, and of Stalinist reconstruction in the East, was over by the late 1960s. The inefficiencies of the bureacratic forms of statism were becoming manifest, and the radical socialist critique, based on workers' democracy and self-management, was outdone by the late 1970s by a new private-capitalist, neo-liberal ideology. The crisis of Western social democracy in the 1980s has now been dwarfed by the complete collapse of Stalinism. The main beneficiary, in the short term at least, is the right-wing market approach, which is gaining a clear political victory in the East and a more muted triumph – given the recession – but a triumph nonetheless in the West.

All this is familiar, but the background is not. What has largely escaped attention is that, with the demise of total war, the economic, social and political basis for mid-century statism has collapsed. From the mid-1950s onwards, nuclear weaponry has had an accelerating influence on war-preparation. Its primary effect has been to demobilize societies: war no longer depends, as it did in 1914–18 and 1939–45, on extensive, and labour-intensive, war industries; on mass armies and conscription; on mass civil defence; on sustained ideological mobilization during years of battles. At the touch of a button, nuclear missiles can achieve all the destruction (and more) that formerly took a massive, ongoing social organization to produce. High-technology weaponry requires large resources, but few people and little mobilization.

The social and political effects of this military transformation have been slower to appear, but even before the end of the Cold War they became decisive. It is no accident that Britain has seen one of the sharpest versions of this experience: the most complete model of 'democratic' mass militarism in 1939–45, it has been since the early 1960s the most completely demobilized, nuclear-reliant of all major states. The exceptionally strong welfare state consensus of the 1940s and 1950s became brittle in the 1970s and 1980s; social participation became dispensable, for the conservative tradition, precisely as and because military participation disappeared.

Statist socialism, in its social democratic as well as Stalinist form, was a variant of the politics of total war. Now that this era is left behind – and the end of the Cold War is the culmination of a historical process spread over the last four decades – socialism can be reconstructed only on a different basis. The socialism of the twenty-first century will not only have to be fundamentally less statist; it will have to settle accounts with the problems of war and militarization which, largely untheorized in the nineteenth century, have bedevilled it in the twentieth.

## Socialism and the international state system

The international system based on competition between states, in which war has been the ultimate mode of conflict resolution, has been characterized by 'realist' international theorists as anarchic. Socialists have generally seen this anarchy as a reflection – or at most a form – of the anarchy of capitalist production with its competitive markets. Socialist solutions to the problems of international anarchy and war have rested on the project of a cooperative socialist commonwealth at a global level.

Socialists have tended, therefore, not to recognize the international state system as distinct from international capitalism. The statism of socialism in political practice corresponds to an under-theorization of the state system in Marxism. Marx, of course, wrote little about it. Later Marxists have generally followed him in writing about 'the state', failing to recognize that capitalism, as a global system, does not have a state, but a competitive state system – which developed from the European state system that preceded capitalist development. Marxist writing about 'the state' has, moreover, tended to reduce it to the results of national class struggles. Lenin's *State and Revolution*, for example, although produced in the depths of the First World War, attributes the 'monstrous, bureaucratic' growth of the state which it describes to the effects of class struggle – rather than to the manifestly more determining militarization which was transforming states and societies on all sides when Lenin wrote.

The revolutionary Marxists of the First World War disagreed in analysing the forms which capitals, states and their rivalries took, and in the explanations which they offered – Lenin, Luxemburg and Bukharin presenting different versions of 'imperialism'. They agreed, however, in ascribing the heightened international anarchy of their times to the intensified competition between corporate capitals. They saw a unified super-imperialism, with a world state, as a theoretical possibility but something which in practice would never be achieved. Bukharin's model of competing 'national state capitalisms', waging fused economic, political and military struggles, was perhaps the most radical in the weight which it gave to inter-state as opposed to inter-capital conflict. It was also the most oversimplified, in seeing the future in terms of endless militarized conflicts between rival capitalist states ('imperialist pirate states') which had converted their economies into state capitalisms and suppressed all democracy.

The political positions which went with these theoretical models of the international system were of course based on class politics, involving the equal rejection of all imperialisms, and a revolutionary attitude towards their conflicts and wars –

to the point of 'defeatism' and the call, as we have seen, for civil war. The emergence of the revolutionary Soviet Union, and its consolidation as a Stalinist state, complicated matters. During the phase of war communism, writers such as Bukharin actually envisaged war between the revolutionary and capitalist states as a higher phase of class struggle. This was perhaps the nadir in the militarization of socialism, although it has had even more alarming echoes in the positions of those socialists who supported Soviet nuclear weapons (the *reductio ad absurdum* of these was the view of a few Trotskyists that a Third World War would offer revolutionary possibilities in the same ways as the First).

It is enough to mention such issues to show that the revolutionary Marxist positions of the early twentieth century cannot be sustained. Indeed this was obvious during the Second World War, when the politicization of international conflict, between Fascist-authoritarian, bourgeois-democratic and Stalinist camps made it impossible to understand the war in simple 'inter-imperialist' terms. The outcome of the war was, moreover, a profound transformation, not only of war itself (due to nuclear weapons) but of the international system. The total defeat of Germany and Japan, the subordination of Britain and other Western European states (whose empires were finally pulled apart in the aftermath), left only the Soviet Union as a counterpoint to American power. The stage was set for the 'bipolar world' which lasted from the late 1940s to the late 1980s.

## The consequences of the Cold War

How we understand the Cold War system is clearly crucial for determining where we are today. Clearly the conflict between the USSR and the West was more than just a conflict of great powers: it was intensified by differences of socio-economic organization, political structure and ideology. Whether, in the end, we see this as deformed socialism, deformed capitalism, or something which was neither one nor the other, is in a sense irrelevant to the effects which its conflict with the mainstream of Western capitalism had on the international system and global society. (In the terms which concerned classical Marxism, it is now apparent that the Stalinist system which prevailed in the USSR and Eastern Europe – versions of which survive only precariously in China, Vietnam, Cuba and North Korea – was a gigantic regional digression rather than a world-historical alternative.)

The Cold War involved, at one level, the simplest possible form of international anarchy, in which only two protagonists counted. This was why it appeared, in the nuclear arms race, as the purest kind of military competition, in which at a certain point technology took over – in an 'exterminist' momentum.[4] It is easy now to discount the dangers of nuclear war, but in the early 1980s, when the USA was installing Pershing II missiles in West Germany which could reach Moscow in under ten minutes, the room for political (let alone economic) calculation in a crisis was fast disappearing.

At other levels, however, the Cold War involved complex political and economic integration. Within each bloc, the Cold War disciplined the subordinate states as well as peoples. This was most obvious in the Soviet bloc, in which the competition with the West was the key lever enabling the Soviet leaders to hold the Eastern European states to the USSR and, through military-patriotic institutions and ideology, the peoples of the USSR to its state. The insuffiency of these imposed military ties, at all levels, and the failure to develop parallel economic and political institutions in effective and legitimate forms, explains much about the eventual collapse of the system.

In the West, the military ties were both more voluntary, on the part of elites but also to some extent electorates, and – crucially – reinforced by political and economic cooperation between states. The central achievement of the Cold War period is that, as a result of the military unity of the West, immense steps forward have been taken in integration of states and economies. Institutionally, of course, this has been taken furthest in Western Europe. Here there has been a striking dialectic of military and political-economic change. Military defeat or weakening of the major European states in the Second World War, and mutual military dependence on the USA in the Cold War, were the essential conditions for the development of European integration. This integration, in turn, has had the effect of eliminating any future possibility of wars between the major European states. This is surely a historic advance of the Cold War period.

This point can be extended – albeit that its longer-term implications are more controversial – to the West as a whole. The military dependence of Japan, Australasia and the newly industrializing states of the Pacific Rim on the USA has been no less profound than that of Western Europe. The development of intra-Western institutions such as NATO, OECD, GATT and the Group of 7 has consolidated an unprecedented degree of political as well as economic interdependence among the major capitalist states. Although these institutions impinge less on the sovereignty of individual states than those of the EU on its members, they represent a parallel integration which embodies the same dialectic that we can see in the EU case. The West's economic integration is predicated on the same military interdependence, and it has the same consequence: that war between the major capitalist blocs (North America, Western Europe, Japan) and between individual Western states in general has become virtually inconceivable.

The point can be extended still further, to the relations between the Cold War adversaries themselves. Although the manifest expression of their conflict was the threat of a nuclear holocaust, the subtext was one of increasing cooperation. The unique circumstance of a prolonged bipolar conflict, mediated by military technology and taking place under conditions of modern bureaucracy and surveillance, enabled the Cold Warriors to engage in unprecedented mutual monitoring. Out of the early phases of the Cold War, rudimentary cooperation developed, so that by the time of the Second Cold War in the 1980s, the USA and USSR maintained extensive, institutionalized contacts.

The latent consequence of the Cold War was therefore a

structure of cooperation between the superpowers, which remains in place with post-Soviet Russia. Indeed what is now happening is that the limited cooperation of the Cold War is being extended into much more inclusive economic and political cooperation – however much the process of extension is fraught with conflicts and contradictions. Although it is obviously too early to see these developments consolidated, the overall result of the Cold War is clear. Although there was a real danger of nuclear war – and we were absolutely right to be concerned about it however small it was – the possibility of war between Russia and the West has now largely been removed. The nationalist reaction which, in late 1993, produced electoral successes for the far right is unlikely to push Russia back into headlong confrontation with the West. Further integration of Russia and other ex-Soviet states with the West, however problematic in economic and political terms, will almost certainly consolidate this extension of peaceful capitalism.

To take this argument further is more difficult, and when we look at Bosnia, Nagorno-Karabakh and Moldova, as well as Cambodia, Liberia, Somalia and other areas of the so-called Third World, it is obvious that the notion of a 'peaceful' post-Cold War world has very definite limits. It is equally obvious that the cooperation among the major capitalist states is often extremely weak, ineffectual and hamfisted when it comes to dealing with such open sores in global society. In no sense can the extension of international institutions such as the UN and the IMF, which incorporate most or all of the world's states, be relied upon to eliminate the dangers of war between them.

We should certainly not minimize these issues, but we should weigh against them the even more crucial gains in the elimination of the danger of major wars, either between the main capitalist states or between East and West. And we should take account of the fact that most major and minor states are closely dependent in myriad ways on Western capitalism, the major Western states and Western-backed international institutions in ways which may often inhibit inter-state wars, although are likely to prove less effective in limiting civil wars or wars resulting from the break-up of multinational states.

We can see this tendency even in an examination of some of the most problematic regions in world politics. China – although its political future is very uncertain – looks for accommodation rather than conflict with the West. The Middle Eastern states, despite their dangerous rivalries, nearly all have some interest in the US-sponsored 'peace process', and armed stalemate – a regional cold war or wars – looks more likely than all-out conflict. Even in Korea, a rapprochement of North and South has begun, even though the cloud of North Korean nuclear weapons hangs over it. In many regions the tensions are real, for state elites, between the benefits of pursuing conflicts with neighbouring states to the point of war and the costs in terms of wider international relations. The end of the Cold War may have opened a Pandora's box of suppressed nationalisms, but it has also removed the powerful stimulus which American-Soviet rivalry provided to regional conflicts, and has substituted the controlling interest of the West in preventing conflicts among clients getting out of hand, and the interests of those clients in gaining what benefits they can from the new Western supremacy.

## The politics of the new world order

The key analytical question is whether the growing economic and political integration of world capitalism, which prevents war among the central states of the system and limits the damage of wars on the margins – from the point of view of the global system if not necessarily for the immediate victims – is likely to be sustained in the longer term. The central political question is whether we should welcome this process, with the new challenges and possibilities which it offers, or reject it as a throwback to untramelled imperialism.

Unreconstructed 'realists' among international relations scholars have been quick to chart the shift from a 'bipolar' to a 'multipolar' world, and to argue the danger of war in Europe and, in the longer term, of armed conflict between a revived Japan and Western Europe and a declining USA. They point, of course, to real issues, but draw misleading conclusions, neglecting the extent to which the shift is to a 'unipolar' *as well as* to a 'multipolar' world. Removing the discipline of the Cold War (and, in the East, of the Stalinist system), does indeed allow old national and inter-state rivalries to revive; and creating new states out of an old empire is frought with dangers of conflict. These processes are unlikely, however, to lead to generalized wars among the major states, and to believe that they will is to ignore the effects of the integrating tendencies which we have just described.

However many local wars are spawned, and however murderous these are for the people involved, they are likely to remain marginal to the new Europe and even more so to the system of Western power as a whole. Where their murderousness becomes too obvious to Western publics, or where – as with the danger of a generalized Balkan war – they threaten to become less marginal, they will now be the object of international interventions, although the rule operating here seems to be, as we shall discuss below, too little and too late.

More critical in the medium and longer term – indeed the central analytical issue which must be resolved – is the balance of power between the main centres of capitalism. It is obvious that the USA is in decline relative, especially, to Japan and other dynamic Asian capitalist economies. Although the Gulf War demonstrated that, for the moment, Japan, like Germany, Saudi Arabia and the Gulf states, was willing to remain America's paymaster, it is indeed likely that at some point early in the next century, at the latest, it will seek political and even military expression of its new power.

Sharper economic and political conflicts between the main capitalist states are certain, now that the constraint of the Cold War is removed; but is there any serious reason to believe that these will or even could take military form? On the contrary, all the signs are that the arguments will be about political (and of course economic) weight within the group of major capitalist states, and hence within the international system as a whole. The military expression of these tensions is likely to concern the role of different states within international peace-keeping – Japan and Germany are edging back towards military recognition in this sense. There is, however, no scenario which is remotely credible in which the armed forces of these states will be pitted again, as they were in the Second World War, against those of the USA, the UK and their allies.

If we reject these scaremongering reactions to current instability, then we are left with the still startling fact that the main tenet of post-Cold War optimism is in fact true: we are now in a world in which, for all its horrifying weaponry and dirty local wars, the prospect of war between the major states in the international system has virtually disappeared. The key political task is to explore the implications of this transformation.

The first consequence is that the politics of disarmament have still a long way to travel. The unravelling of the nuclear arms race, and of the military establishments of the Cold War taken as a whole, has hardly begun. Many political and military leaders are no doubt looking for new 'threats' to justify maintaining their forces, and it it is clear that it will take some years for the full implications of the historic change to be realized. There can be little doubt, however, that in the long run it will not be possible for states to justify maintaining even trimmed-down Cold War military establishments, when the Cold War has receded into history and no big substitute for it has been found. The forces required for 'peacekeeping', although substantial, are very different in quality and quantity from those required for an East-West war. Nuclear weapons are notably redundant. Here is a remarkable opportunity to replace the politics of military defence and deterrence with a politics of security based on international cooperation and addressing global inequalities.

The second result is that the politics of war will cease to be about East-West rivalry, and will now become almost exclusively the politics of global 'policing' and 'peacekeeping'. There will be a complex range of issues, the scope of which is already becoming apparent, from the Ulsters, ex-Yugoslavias and Nagorno-Karabakhs, through the Cambodias, Somalias and Iraqs, to the management of massively armed rivalries in the Middle East. At one end of the range are the conflicts of irregularly armed ethnic groups in regions where statehood is precarious; at the other end are conflicts of major regional states in some of which nuclear weapons could become involved. Tied up with these problems, of course, are issues of arms production and supply, which connect directly with political and economic issues in the advanced countries. The whole policing/peacekeeping problematic, moreover, is the new bottom line for the structures and levels of military organization (and expenditure) in Western states.

At the centre of the new wars, most of which arise from ethnic and/or national conflicts within states, or between neighbouring states, are threats to civilian populations. Control over territory focuses on ethnic composition, and, although the language of 'ethnic cleansing' arises from the ex-Yugoslav wars, the pattern of genocidal war, aimed at removing people of distinct ethnic origins from a given territory, is common to many cases in Asia and Africa as well as on the eastern and southern edges of Europe. The new wars therefore primarily involve, from the point of view of Western civil society if not Western states, the issue of the protection of civilians. The question which arises is that of how far Western-led intervention (military as well as political), under UN auspices, can actually protect populations at risk.

The left is likely to have more difficulties with this set of issues than with the more straightforward (especially nuclear) disarmament issues, although ultimately they are related. At base the issue is whether the imposition of a 'global consensus' by a US-led coalition of Western states, albeit supported by Russia and China and many other states and mobilized through international institutions, can be supported in any sense, however critically and conditionally. Clearly the specific interests of the dominant partners in this coalition will tend to predominate, leading to selectivity in the cases, levels and forms of intervention. The contrast between Western (and hence UN) responses to the Gulf and ex-Yugoslav crises clearly manifests this. The arrogance and electoral opportunism of declining American (and British) power, whether manifested in abuse of its Japanese paymasters, the cynical manipulation of the Iraqi Kurds and Shi'as, or the deep hypocrisy which has surrounded the Bosnian intervention, will raise many hackles among its allies, as well as on the left.

A third effect is that the role of militarism in society and culture will be radically transformed. Already, during the Cold War, all the Western states 'offshore' from the European continent (USA, UK, Japan, Australia, Canada, New Zealand) have dispensed with conscription. In Western Europe (as in the USSR and Eastern Europe) military service remained, but the historic link between military service and citizenship has been progressively attenuated, with increasing provision of non-military alternatives (in Germany over one third of young men opt for civilian service although it involves a longer term). Western societies have become more 'post-military', with a militarism of the media rather than mass participation, a trend which is likely to be greatly accelerated in the post-Cold War years. Already, century-old traditions of military service are in question in both Eastern and Western Europe. This creates historic possibilities for a democratic culture with post-military citizenship.[5]

These changes in the social and cultural significance of militarism, taken together with the shift from nuclear armaments towards global policing and peacemaking, imply a very different context for the politics of war. There is a possibility for an anti-war politics to gain support in increasingly demilitarized societies. At the same time, however, there are difficult dilemmas, in that political intervention by international institutions or Western powers is generally not carried out early enough to pre-empt local or civil wars, and that, once these conflicts are under way, only military intervention may offer any real possibility of inhibiting vicious local or civil wars. The idea of war to prevent war has always seemed dangerous, and today's situation – even though military interventions occur under the auspices of international institutions – is no exception.

## The Gulf and the new politics of war

The Gulf War raised the new politics of war in a sharp form, but the left as a whole did not give a clear answer. Did the fact that Western interests in oil were clearly involved negate the case for intervention against a state which had committed very blatant aggression against another (and indeed had done the same against Iran only nine years earlier)? Did the fact that there had been no international intervention against other, more pro-Western invaders fatally weaken the case for intervention against Iraq? Much of the left opposed the war, but it hardly resolved these issues, nor was it clear whether opposition concerned international intervention as such, the fact that it was occurring under US leadership, or the forms which it was taking – sanctions, military reinforcement of Saudi Arabia, and finally war against Iraq. Was the left opposing the war because it objected to its political basis, or because it objected to the means of international discipline against Iraq – to war in general, or to the particular kind of war which was launched?

How difficult it is for the left to break with knee-jerk anti-Americanism and anti-imperialism was seen in the often abusive reactions to the 'apostasy' of Fred Halliday.[6] Many critics used a high moral tone – his 'disregard' for loss of life – to underscore a basically political objection to a pro-US position. The moral tone was often out of place, since the critics themselves would have been happy to support (revolutionary) war in other contexts. It was also beside the point to charge 'betrayal', on this moral issue at least, since Halliday's 'realism' in supporting US military action to defeat Iraq was of a piece with his earlier Marxist realism in supporting revolutionary war where necessary.

Halliday's position on the Gulf bares the two central dilemmas in dealing with the 'new international order'. On the one hand, there is the issue of whether, in the last analysis, to support international policing under UN auspices, even where its scope and form are highly coloured by US or Western interests, and have overtones of 'super-imperialism'. On the other hand, there is the issue of war: is it generally, or in specific cases, justified as a means of such policing? Halliday, in the Gulf case, took these two issues together and answered 'yes' to both. While it is certainly correct that the issues are linked, the connection may be less one-dimensional than Halliday's position suggests. Instead, we may answer 'yes' and 'no', respectively, both in the specific case of the Gulf and in general.

To elaborate: global policing, to ensure the increasing development and application of international law and standards, is essential, and it is unavoidable that it is developed, at best through a reformed UN, largely in ways that will be proposed by the major Western states. It does not follow, however, that all-out war is an appropriate means of policing. In the case of Kuwait, it is arguable first that a more politically interventionist policy on the part of the USA, the Western world and the UN might have prevented the Iraqi occupation; secondly that sanctions, reinforced by a military blockade and deterrent forces in Saudi Arabia, although offering no certain outcome, represented a formidable means of pressure on the Iraqi regime; and last but not least, that the costs of the US-led assault for the Iraqi (especially Kurdish and Shi'a) people outweighed any possible benefits in punishing an aggressor state, or for the people of occupied Kuwait.

These issues need to be historically contextualized in an analysis of the changes in the international system and the role of war in general. The most important point is that the creeping abolition of war, as a means of resolving conflicts between the major capitalist states, is an immense gain in every sense. It removes the danger of the nuclear annihilation of human civilization, and with it the lurking fear which has poisoned culture for four decades. It creates the possibility that resources can be transferred from war-preparation to peaceful uses. How important this gain is, if also how fragile, is surely demonstrated by the horrors we have seen even in the relatively small-scale, partly irregular wars in ex-Yugoslavia, Somalia,

Armenia-Azerbaijan and elsewhere. It is important to consolidate this gain in a politics which emphasizes that war in general is unacceptable; the onus must be on those who advocate a particular war to argue an exception from this general norm.[7] The use of military force in peacekeeping and even peacemaking, while inevitably crossing the line into war, must be kept as clearly distinguished as possible from it.

The creation of a politically unified capitalist world has other, more specifically political, benefits. It reduces the significance of inter-state rivalries as a political factor. Nationalism remains a vibrant force, of course, in the advanced Western countries as well as the newly liberated East, but where it can no longer lead to war its edge is fundamentally blunted. The integrative tendencies of modernity mean that issues of international cooperation, coordination and intervention are central as never before. The possibilities for developing and popularizing a democratic and socialist agenda – for strengthening human rights and democratic control, for reducing international inequalities, for ensuring basic standards of life in all regions, for addressing global environmental issues – are far greater in this context.

For the left, this is particularly important. It has suffered historic defeats because the forces unleashed by war have been far stronger than those of labour movements. Socialism has lost out because the divisions between states have been seen as of greater importance than the divisions within societies. It has been crippled by statist and militarizing ideas, originating in processes of war mobilization for which socialist ideas provided little understanding. The history of twentieth-century socialism has been dominated by the processes, which are deeply rooted in the historical contexts in which capitalist industrialism developed in the nineteenth. The emancipation of the core areas of capitalism from the threat of total war is a historic change of the first order.

In these circumstances, we cannot but welcome the trends towards international integration, political as well as economic, and the rise of a new interventionism. The historic dangers lie not in these trends, but in a new fragmentation. If the USA retreats into isolationism; if the EU fails to maintain a momentum for union; if the UN fails to develop as a more responsible global institution: then we shall have greater cause to worry. If the responses to crises of all of these are so weak and divided that local wars go unchecked; economic, social and political disintegration in the East spirals down; global environmental problems, and global inequalities, remain un-addressed: then the prospects for a socialist and democratic agenda will be far poorer. The present situation in Western politics, in which petty nationalisms and local economic concerns predominate, is a warning of this downside.

The tasks of socialists in the post-Cold War era are to work with the internationalizing and interventionist forces in capital-ism, and through democratic political action to develop a different agenda and priorities for the international system. The 'new world order' does not belong to the USA, to the West, or even just to states. It is an increasingly pluralist system of states, and one in which the traditional divides between international politics and national politics, between the affairs of states and those of peoples, are breaking down. The possibilities for political action and social movements to influence international politics have been demonstrated, as we saw in Chapter 3, in the roles of Western European peace movements and Eastern European democratic movements in ending the Cold War – as well as negatively by the often destructive role of popular nationalism. The democratic left can help to mould the new world system if it participates in opening up these new possibilities with its own agenda.

The reshaping of socialist politics for a twenty-first century world, in which war between the major states is no longer a danger, will involve many issues which have already been debated. Attitudes to democracy and markets, global in-equalities and ecology, will obviously be crucial, but a clear, historically framed attitude to war is equally important. If war has become redundant between major states in the centre of the international system, war on the periphery, in terms of national/ethnic struggles, inter-state conflicts and Western/ international intervention, is now an increasingly critical issue.

It is essential to clarify both the basic concepts and the ground-rules which apply to these wars.

## The historical redundancy of war

The concept of the historical redundancy of war, which is increasingly accepted in the context of relations between the advanced industrial states, applies increasingly on a global scale. Most obviously, the proliferation of nuclear weapons capability means that the destructive potential of regional wars is approaching the same mutually self-defeating dead end in which the East-West conflict ended. At the lower levels of international politics and of destructiveness, it is still true that war offers many potential gains for states and proto-state movements: but we should act *as if* the historical redundancy of war applied in these cases too. This is because such wars cause immense suffering; because they block economic and political progress; because they often produce militarized and authoritarian regimes; and because they can still have a destabilizing impact on larger regional conflicts and the wider international system.

Such a perspective means that the left should abandon some of the political positions of the recent past, and especially its twin belief that wars of national liberation are automatically progressive and Western interventions in the Third World automatically bad. It means adopting a perspective on any form of military action with an inbuilt assumption that war and violence are outmoded and self-defeating means; where they can be justified, this must be argued as an exception to a rule of 'historical pacifism'. This standard must be applied to 'liberation' struggles, and the lessons learnt from cases like those of Czechoslovakia, with its Velvet Revolution, South Africa, where political struggle is pushing forward where the bomb failed, and Ireland, where the armed struggle acts as a permanent block to any political solution. The arming of the Bosnian government forces, for example, was no substitute for greater UN intervention to stop the war in Bosnia in 1992–3.

The same standard of the redundancy of war must apply, however, to international interventions as well as to the actions of states and political movements. In a world bristling with military power of all kinds, it is alas unrealistic to believe that the dangers of war can always be averted without resort to military power on the part of those who wish to prevent it. The insertion of UN forces into ex-Yugoslavia, Cambodia or Nagorno-Karabakh may be a necessary means of limiting appalling destruction. 'Peacekeeping' has been the Cinderella of military power in the last forty years, but it deserves a great deal of thought as well as additional resources in the future. Political and where necessary military intervention on behalf of international agencies, with the object of preventing or stopping war, should be a norm rather than an exception, but the tradition of non-aggression should be maintained. It is important that the actions of UN forces are models of restraint in the deployment of military force.

The distinction needs to be made, therefore, between the principles of 'peacekeeping' and 'policing', and the resort to all-out war in the pursuit of these aims. It is here that Halliday's dual position on the Gulf needs to be uncoupled. It was right that a firm international political stance was taken against Iraq, since blatant military aggression is incompatible with any international order, let alone a newly peaceful world. It was extremely positive that virtually all states complied with UN sanctions against Iraq (even if we may argue about the effects on the Iraqi population of the kinds of sanctions imposed), making them unprecedentedly successful. It was justified for the USA to send military forces to Saudi Arabia, as there was a real if small risk that Iraq would extend its aggression. What was more dubious was the early choice by the American government of war against Iraq, before the medium-term effects of sanctions were known.

It is argued (with justification) that there was no certainty, or even reasonable probability, that sanctions would have compelled Iraq to withdraw from Kuwait. According to the criteria offered here, however, the onus was on those who advocated war to prove that this was the only viable course, the effects of which would be superior to those of sanctions. It is certainly arguable that the slow erosion of Saddam Hussein's position by sanctions might have been more damaging to him than the polarizing effects of war, which consolidated his position in the ruling elite (he also chose war). The suffering of the remaining inhabitants of Kuwait was made worse, in the short term, while appalling suffering was undoubtedly caused both directly and indirectly to Iraqi civilians, and notably the Shi'ite and Kurdish minorities. This is not to mention the wholesale killing of Iraqi troops, many of whom belonged to these same minorities. In addition, we should take into account the environmental damage. The restoration of Kuwait was achieved, but at great cost. We may add to these direct factors (last but not least) the damage that was done to the emerging culture of peace by the media coverage of a 'successful' war.

The Gulf War cast a great shadow over the hopes for post-Cold War peace. At the same time, looking to the future, the most dangerous regional military power in the world (Iraq had already precipitated the war with Iran, the bloodiest since Vietnam) has indeed been weakened, even if this might have been achieved by other means. Precedents have been established in the international inspection and destruction of weaponry, including nuclear weapons, and in intervention (however limited) to protect threatened minorities. The USA has been able to exert greater leverage on Middle Eastern states, raising hopes – if not of a genuine peace settlement – of preventing further highly dangerous wars between states in the region.

The ex-Yugoslav crisis raises these issues in a very different form, since all-out war has been the last thing that Western states have wished to wage there. The West has clarified the principles which should govern the situation – respect for both inter-republican borders and the rights of minorities, non-recognition of territorial gains or population movements achieved by force – only after Serbian aggression has made these almost unachievable. It may be that, once the war got under way, the only way to obtain any approximation to these admirable principles was, in fact, by greater Western military involvement. If the West had actively intervened, politically, to attempt to oversee the post-communist restructuring of Yugoslavia and insist on the principles now elaborated, two or three years ago, war might have been averted. If only the West had given priority to political solutions of the Kosovo and Macedonian problems (which at the time of writing seem potentially very dangerous), it would be more likely that we will avoid the wider Balkan war which everyone must fear.

The ex-Yugoslav situation underlines, then, the case for international policing in a political sense, while it makes no case for the resort to all-out war (no one can believe that a Baghdad-style bombardment of Belgrade would help the victims of Serbian aggression in Bosnia or Croatia). It focuses attention on the variety of roles for 'limited' military action to support international political intervention: on the range of options from the protection of UN monitors and relief convoys, to which the Western powers have reluctantly agreed, through to air power or large ground forces to protect civilian populations and establish 'safe havens', or even to push back the Serbian occupiers of large parts of Bosnia.

There are no easy answers to these questions. The crucial point for socialists is that they define a new political debate, in which nation-states are subject to international standards of democracy, human rights, minority rights, etc.; the institutions of the world order are increasingly seen as existing to uphold such standards; and military power is legitimated only in so far as it plays a constructive part in achieving these ends. Correspondingly, therefore, there is a new military debate (or in conventional terms 'defence debate') in which the politics of global policing, peacekeeping and peacemaking rather than Cold War increasingly defines an instrinsically more limited role for military power.

## Socialist voices in the new debates

Socialism may seem so discredited that socialist voices may appear to have little to offer in these new debates. And yet they may have much to offer, as long as they recognize clearly how the world, and the arguments, have changed. The critiques of capitalist power are still relevant, but their significance is transformed by the new situation. If it is not viable to denounce each and every Western intervention as 'imperialist', it is still relevant to criticize where specific interests – whether it be in oil or electoral success – distort the priorities of Western states. More fundamentally, we need a critique of the ways in which the major Western states have resisted endowing international institutions with real substance, have refused to give real priority to means of anticipating international difficulties, still cling too much to the idea of national 'sovereignty', and above all react to crises too little, too unimaginatively and too late.

The socialist tradition was, before its statization by war, a thoroughly societally based politics. It can still offer, positively, the idea that international policy must be based on a thoroughgoing attempt to redress global inequalities; to attack global environmental problems; to institute democratic principles, including human rights, protection for minorities and political democracy, at the heart of international interventions; and to minimize the use of military violence. While all these ideas are paid lip service in mainstream liberal-democratic debate – and thus establish a common field of argument – all of them are thoroughly compromised or downgraded in the practice of Western states. Socialists should be their most consistent and enthusiastic advocates at every turn.

Socialists ought, indeed, to be the most insistent on the new context. If anything is left of socialism, it must surely be its critical capacity, the ability to criticize mercilessly what exists, and to see realities in a comprehensive historical perspective. The historical irony of the Cold War is that it has created the possibility of a peaceful international system. If this possibility is turned into a more lasting reality in the twenty-first century, it may make it possible to renew the agenda of social transformation after its war-marked historic defeats in the twentieth.

## NOTES

1 The general argument developed in this section follows my *Dialectics of War*. For a closer historical discussion of its political significance, see my 'Marxism, War and Peace in Britain, 1895–1945'. In Richard Taylor and Nigel Young, eds, *Campaigns for Peace*, Manchester: Manchester University Press, 1987, pp. 49–72. For an exploration in relation to peace movement thinking, see my 'Exterminism and historical pacifism'. In Harvey Kaye, ed., *E. P. Thompson: Critical Debates*, Cambridge: Polity, 1990, pp. 233–51.

2 I have developed this argument further in *Dialectics of War*.

3 See my *Socialism and Militarism*, Nottingham: Spokesman, 1981.

4 See E. P. Thompson, 'Notes on exterminism, the highest stage of civilisation', and consequent discussion, in Thompson et al, *Exterminism and Cold War*, London: Verso, 1982.

5 See my *Post-Military Society*, chapter 5.

6 Halliday's position is outlined, for example, in 'The crisis of the Arab world: the false answers of Saddam Hussein', *New Left Review*, 184, Nov–Dec 1990, pp. 69–75, and 'The left and war', *New Statesman and Society*, 8 March 1991, pp. 15–16; see also the letters by Robin Blackburn and others, *New Statesman and Society*, 22 March 1991, pp. 30–2, and Norman Geras, 'The fudge of war', *New Statesman and Society*, 29 March 1991, p. 14.

7 For further exposition of this argument, see my *Dialectics of War*, ch. 5, pp. 101–42.

*Seven*

# Towards Global Responsibility

We have discussed in Chapter 6 how the politics of war have been transformed, and historic positions outmoded, by the transformations of the international system. Although the argument so far has been informed by a global society perspective, it has not fully confronted its political implications. Nor has it addressed the issues of agency which are central to the tension between global society and traditional international relations approaches. In this final chapter, the aim is to look at these issues directly, and to draw together conclusions from the various stages of the critique in this book.

International relations has traditionally centred, as we have seen, on conceptions of state security understood as national security. Recent writers, as we saw in Chapter 4, have distinguished between national and international security, the latter being understood as the security of the state system or the society of states as a whole. This concept has, of course, its corollary in practical politics in the idea of the international community, which has been much invoked since 1989. Like the concepts of national security, international security is, however, a statist concept.

International theory has also generated concepts of the individual, and more radically of community in the broadest sense, as alternative foundations of international politics, as well as more limited societal translations of state or national security interests. These are important developments, but we have argued that the debate needs placing on firmer foundations, deriving from a perspective on global society. Only in this sense can we develop a sociologically secure approach to contemporary world politics. It is now time to explore the implications of this perspective.

## The politics of global civil society

The emergence of global society has been, as we argued in Chapter 1, an uneven and contradictory process. The development of civil society at a global level is still more problematic and uncertain. The future of world politics depends a great deal, however, on the growth of global civil society, and this must be the starting point for a new politics of the international.

It is increasingly clear that at the end of the twentieth there is a widespread dissolution of existing state forms, as well as of the dominant patterns of the state system. Some multinational states such as the Soviet Union and Yugoslavia have fallen apart in destructive and warlike ways; others such as Czechoslovakia have broken up more peacefully. Within seemingly more homogenous nation-states, however, and not only in Eastern Europe and Africa, but in the advanced West too (for example, Italy, Belgium, Canada), the same pressures towards fragmentation have been felt, even if they have been managed for the most part without violence.

It is less clearly seen, perhaps, that the decline of centralized national (and, still more, multinational) states is mirrored in the crisis of national civil societies. This crisis takes different forms, of course: in former communist and Third World totalitarian states, civil society has been weak and suppressed. There the crisis is one of the character and integrity of the emerging civic culture and institutions, which are widely threatened by economic crisis and corruption as well as by the political crudeness, authoritarianism and in many cases violence of ethnic nationalism.

In the West, however, where civil society has historically been strong, it is also in crisis. Here the crisis is one of decay, as the historic traditions and institutions of national democracies atrophy. The most visible manifestation of crisis is the widely remarked disillusion with political leaders across the Western world which has grown apace in the years since 1989. Beneath this, however, are deeper and longer-term trends, as well as a wider specific crisis of the post-Cold War years. The decline of class-based political parties and social movements, especially the labour movements, has been a feature of the last three decades, since their post-Second World War peak. It is not only political parties and trade unions which have declined, however; the other main institutions of civil society have been equally decisively undermined. Mainstream churches have, for the most part, continued to decay. The civic traditions of municipalities have lost much of their vibrancy. Intelligentsias have been institutionalized in universities and have lost much of their critical function.

The crisis of Western civil society has been gathering pace, therefore, for several decades and it has deep structural roots. Changes in production have dispersed the large concentrations of workers which were formed in the nineteenth and early twentieth centuries. Changes in transportation and housing have dispersed the great urban and metropolitan populations. The growth of mass communications has transformed the cultural universe, facilitating the privatization of social life. Under the Cold War umbrella which brought Western states closer, the nationalisms which formerly held civil societies together ideologically have also declined.

The crisis of Western civil society assumes a particularly sharp form at the end of the twentieth century. The Cold War may have constituted a framework for the decay of civil society, but at least it was a framework, in which institutions and ideologies continued to function. With its removal, it is as if the ideological cement of Western civil societies has dissolved. Politicians lose their last semblance of ideological respectability and are exposed as self-seeking and ineffectual manipulators. The opinion poll ratings of governments and statesmen hit rock-bottom, while mainstream oppositions often fail to capitalize on their unpopularity. Liberal ideology quickly sheds its 1989–90 aura of triumphalism and appears incapable of managing the world crisis. Social democracy, instead of renewing itself with the demise of its communist rival, appears blighted by disillusion with all forms of socialism and, even more, irrelevant to the new times. Even the Green parties and the new social movements appear debilitated in the new situation.

With the decline of the historic institutions and ideologies of civil society, the mass media assume an even more critical role. The media become, indeed, the main fora of civil society, the means through which society is reflected and reflects upon itself. To the extent that the old institutions of civil society continue to respond at all, they are increasingly dependent on the media for their ability to project themselves. The old roots of parties, churches and unions in local, regional and national activity and organizations, while still a routine part of their functioning, are less and less significant to their success or failure. The media become the focus of fierce contestation, both from the state and civil society, and from within, as differentiations in approach and style between and within media institutions become critical reflections of the choices facing society.

The crisis of Western civil society is a central part of the problem of global civil society, but it is only one part. Certainly, the development of global civil society must depend in large measure on the ability of civil society in the West to renew itself. Although the decay is serious, there are a tradition and an understanding of the role of civil society, and the general economic as well as cultural resources, which are necessary to the creation of a global civil society. The dominant role of the West in global society, economically, politically and culturally, means that its role is central. The situation of civil society in the West is profoundly affected, however, by the larger global context. Its crisis is in part a crisis of confidence in the global role of Western civilization and values. This aspect has been enormously magnified since 1989.

Global civil society is beginning to emerge partly as a result of the interaction of Western and non-Western civil societies in the global crises of the late twentieth century. As state institutions are thrown into crisis, especially in regions of Eastern Europe, Asia and Africa, the pre-existing local forms of civil society, and indeed in some areas the very existence of society, are brought into question. Communities – families, villages and towns, ethnic groupings, their ways of life, traditions and forms of social organization – are threatened, along with the lives and well-being of individuals. A contest begins, not just between rival nationalisms, but between exclusivist, authoritarian, ethnic-nationalist and inclusivist, globalist, democratic and pluralist versions of civil society. In some of the most brutal civil wars (for example, Bosnia), the latter are likely to be almost extinguished, and caricatures of the historic mid-twentieth-century nationalisms reinstated. Elsewhere, however, forms of civil society which – even if limited – are more open and democratic than those which have previously existed may come into existence.

These vital tests of the creation or development of civil society in the former East and South are equally critical challenges to the vitality of civil society in the West. What is at stake are the values of civil society as they have developed in the Western world. Either these values are strengthened, renewed and expanded in their area of influence on a global scale, or the decay of the historic forms of Western civil society is underlined with the defeat of the new growths of civil society in non-Western arenas.

The concept of global civil society is thus proposed in an extreme critical tension with current historical developments. The formation of global civil society depends on the growth of a moral, intellectual and political culture linking the fragile and threatened civil societies of East and South with the historic but decaying civil societies of the West. It depends too on the renewal of institutions in civil society and the emergence of movements expressing the values of globalism. So far these tendencies can be identified only in very limited forms.

Just as mass media of communication constitute, we argued

above, increasingly central institutions of Western civil society, so they also form foci of the globalization of civil society. Media communicate not only information about world events, but also the debates about how 'we', as individuals, societies and states, should respond. The self-styled 'global' media – CNN supplying every national news network as well as every hotel bedroom – are less important than the global flows between national and regional television and newspapers.

The other foci of the emerging global civil society appear more uncertain. The decay of traditional (national) forms of Western civil society has equally involved, even more sharply, the decay of international social and political movements, most notably of the international labour movement. The new global social movements, most notably the environmental movement, are still weaker in terms of sustained mass participation and institutional development than the old labour movements in their heyday. Many agencies have developed which operate within civil society and link the East and the South with the West through humanitarian, development and civil rights as well as environmental issues. Few of these agencies are organized as fully democratic movements, however, and most allocate their supporters the role of donors and their beneficiaries the role of recipients. Only very modest beginnings exist for the democratic political formations which would express the new global links of civil society, but the building of these formations is a central project of our times.

## Global state institutions and their interventions

The weak institutions of global civil society correspond, of course, to weak global state institutions. As international theorists rarely tire of reminding us, the international system is a system of states, and such international or global institutions as exist are still predominantly extensions of this system. The principal international organization, the United Nations, is – as its name suggests – a conglomerate of nation-states, in which voting takes place on the basis of states and the rights of sovereign states are recognized above those of individuals and social groups.

It would clearly be foolish to ignore or deny these realities. Any realistic analysis of the operation of international institutions – including other global and regional organizations as well as the UN – must accept the basic fact that they depend primarily on nation-states for their decisions, resources and policy implementation. In the end, a few powerful, chiefly Western, states – often ultimately the United States – determine the most crucial decisions, even if other states and non-state institutions have a limited influence.

Despite these manifest limitations, from the perspective of global society it is clearly important to underline the fact that the UN and other international institutions are more than simple extensions of states. They can also be seen as embryonic global state institutions, with growing autonomy, however tenuous this may seem at times, from nation-states. Recent developments in the post-Cold War UN may have underlined the force of the realist view which emphasizes the organization's limitations and its dependence on the major powers. These developments have also seen the UN increasingly responding, however problematically, as a global organization to perceived global crisis.

While formally the UN's various interventions have usually been based on definitions of crisis in international security, seen as the security of states, in reality its actions have frequently been driven by recognition of human and social crises. The UN's remit has been affected by the emergence of civil society connections, mediated by mass communications, which reverberate in the politics of nation-states. What is most remarkable is the way in which the concepts of state sovereignty and non-intervention in the affairs of sovereign states have become attenuated in practice – if not yet very far in theory. There is increasingly widespread recognition that these concepts cannot be sustained, in any simple, traditional sense, in many circumstances.

It is easy to dismiss, from a realist or Marxist point of view perhaps, the significance of this shift, and certainly narrow definitions of state interests prevail sufficiently to make most UN proclamations of humanitarian or social concern seem hollow if not hypocritical. From the perspective of an emergent global civil society, however, these developments are crucial markers for the future. They indicate, perhaps only symbolically for the time being – but symbols are important – the way in which international state institutions are in the process of transformation from narrow extensions of national state interests to state organizations of the developing global society.

The crucial question here is that of accountability of the UN and other international organizations to civil society. Clearly, in the present period the UN is formally accountable only to states, and this is unlikely to change in the foreseeable future (although, at a regional level, the partial accountability of the European Union to the European Parliament has set a symbolically important precedent of more direct electoral accountability for international organizations). Indirectly and informally, however, it is clear that the UN is becoming responsive to what is seen as international public opinion, that is, the pressure of views emerging from within civil society. The haphazard nature of this responsiveness, or the fact that it is mediated by the policies of the major Western states, should not mask the equally important fact that the pressure increasingly arises from common responses to commonly perceived issues, across numbers of states, increasingly made effective at a global level.

The issue which arises here is that of the international state system as a whole, and international institutions as the common forms of that system, beginning to function as the state institutions of global society and to be responsive – indeed even accountable – to that society. Clearly we are in the very early stages of the process, in which it is barely recognizable and easily overshadowed by other, more familiar tendencies. We are still very far from the old dreams (or nightmares) of world government. A historic change is taking place nevertheless, and it is important to ask where it might and indeed should lead.

It is particularly important to consider the other side of the relationship between global state institutions and global society, namely the 'intervention' of the former in the latter. This issue arises, in the mid-1990s, primarily in the form of military intervention, which is considered in more detail below. The fact that the issue arises in this form is in itself an index of the primitive nature of global state intervention compared with state intervention in the national context. Nation-states, at least where these are advanced and consolidate, rarely use military power to intervene within society, but manage their interventions through political, socio-economic, cultural and ideological surveillance. It is a reflection of the weakness of global state institutions, and the fact that they are often pressed to intervene in regions where state institutions themselves are weak and unsophisticated, that military intervention largely proceeds or displaces other forms of intervention.

The fact that military intervention is the most visible form of global intervention should not allow us, however, to conflate the two. On the contrary, it is essential to examine the issue of intervention in general, and to discuss the relationships between the military and other forms of intervention.

## Global state intervention and society

The concept of intervention implies some form of externality of the intervener to the intervened-upon. In the discussion of international intervention, the externality in question is generally assumed to be in relation to national boundaries. What is in question is the intervention of other states, or of international institutions, in the affairs of a given state and national society.

While this dimension is by definition present in global state intervention – and within the account given so far there is a large issue of the relationship between the interventions of states and of international institutions, to which we shall return – there is a more fundamental aspect to consider.

Global state intervention is not merely a state–state relationship, but a state–society relationship, and as such should be seen as merely one form of state intervention in general.

The problem here, perhaps, is that state intervention is out of fashion, politically and intellectually. The retreat of statism from its early post-1945 high-point has left the idea of state intervention weak and discredited. There are few quarters in which it is still believed that a far-sighted and socially motivated state apparatus can remould economy and society in progressive terms. On all sides, there is a new belief in the role of 'spontaneous' social and economic forces, as opposed to state action.

This political-intellectual shift, however, is far from a simple negation of the statist momentum of the epoch of total war. On the contrary, the core of what has been known as state intervention – if not the concept itself – remains at the heart of all forms of political economy. Everywhere state management of the economy and society is now so much an integral part of established systems that while its forms – for example, the direct state ownership of industries and services which was widely established after 1945 – may be transformed, the substance remains ever more central. If, indeed, the concept of state intervention is outmoded at the nation-state level, it is because the state is now so internal to most economic and social relations that it is difficult to see in what sense it is still valid to talk of intervention.

This takes us to the heart of the problem of intervention. The externality of the classic concept of state intervention is that of the state in relation to civil society. While the distinction can still and still needs to be made, in reality, however, the boundaries have become less and less clear-cut. The extension and sophistication of surveillance means that there are no spheres of civil society in which the state is not implicated. It should not be thought, however, that this is a one-way process. There is a corresponding civilization of the state, in which particular branches of the state apparatus are intensively monitored by civil institutions and social groups who are implicated in their activities. In this way state intervention, while never losing the capacity for arbitrariness on which much of its bad reputation rests, is nevertheless domesticated or civilized – that is, managed at least partially in the interests of civil society.

The problem of global state intervention is that it has hardly begun to develop in this way. At base this reflects the mutual and symbiotic weakness of global state institutions and global civil society. Whereas nation-states have developed over many centuries, international institutions are of comparatively recent growth and are still very much weaker than nation-states. International institutions are still overwhelmingly dependent on the system of nation-states for their legitimacy, and even more on a relatively small number of powerful states for their resources. It is not surprising that international intervention is still regarded – in many quarters across the globe and across the political spectrum – as archetypically external in a doubly negative sense.

In the critics' eyes, global state intervention compounds the problems of externality, imposition and arbitrariness associated with state intervention in general because, of course, of the additional dimension of extra-nationality. It is manifestly true that international institutions are generally at one or more further removes than nation-state institutions from the face-to-face social relationships and the lived culture of most people. These institutions are notorious for their quintessentially remote bureaucracies and difficulties of multi-linguistic communication.

International institutions, whatever their inherent problems and current inadequacies, have, however, developed for good reasons. These reasons are, in essence, all to do with the globalization of social life which we have discussed. Indeed, it is manifestly the case that the globalization of state organization is very weakly developed in comparison with that of society in general. This weakness may, to some eyes, be a virtue, but there is a strong case to be made for the necessity of their further development. The schemers for world government, much derided though they have been in recent decades, had a very real point, the validity of which is increasing apace.

A global society necessarily implies global institutions, global regulation, global surveillance. We know now that a single global state will not spring onto the scene in one bound, but we are all equally surely aware of the rapid and unavoidable extension of state organization at a global level.

We have also learnt to avoid evolutionary perspectives on social life. We may say by way of analogy, however, that we are now in some ways (if not all) at a comparable stage in the growth of global state organization and intervention to that reached, say, 100 to 150 years ago in terms of Western nation-states and their interventions. What I mean is that there are the same depths of social crisis; the same potential for state intervention as a means of tackling them; and the same fundamental refusal of those holding state power to envisage transformation. There are also, perhaps, some of the same difficulties in developing and implementing change.

The global crises of economy, environment and human rights – not to mention war – are on a monumental scale. No one can seriously believe that they will be resolved spontaneously as a result of market forces, purely local political settlements and bilateral agreements among states. In those cases in which progress has been made towards a resolution of longstanding conflicts – South Africa, Israel and the Palestinians, etc. – these processes have only succeeded so far as they have through sustained international involvement at both state and civil society levels. Where modest steps have been taken to tackle fundamental environmental problems – global warming, ozone depletion – it has been by global political agreement. Such limited steps as have been taken to tackle deepening global economic inequalities depend intimately on the regimes of global economic regulation – on GATT, on the decisions of the Group of 7, etc.

It is enough to mention these cases, however, to realize that, while the development of global political, environmental and economic management is needed, it has so far been very little developed in comparison with its potential. The reasons for this are clearly to do with the limited interests – or conceptions of interests – of the great powers both in tackling such problems and in developing global institutions. It is sometimes argued that the lesser, Third World states could use international fora such as the United Nations to further this case, but they often have even stronger interests than Western states in blocking the development of global institutions – fearing, for example, the extension of monitoring of individual and minority rights and inhibitions on the development and use of military power.

Within global society, therefore, we need a conception and a programme of global responsibility, in which it is accepted that there is both interest in and moral obligation towards the well-being of fellow human-beings across the world with whom we share an increasingly common social life. First of all, we need a programme of economic responsibility, to attack the global recession, to tackle the fundamental issue of global redistribution, to put aid and development politics into first place, to address the economic transition in the former communist states, and to ensure that economic development is compatible with environmental safety. Secondly, we require a programme of political responsibility to uphold democracy, minority and individual rights across the world, and to require states to match the pious declarations which they have signed with real guarantees of freedom. Thirdly, we require a programme of responsibility in international relations, to ensure that states behave towards one another in terms of rules which respect one another's rights and those of their peoples.

To institute such a programme requires comprehensive and sustained intervention by global authorities in regional and national affairs. It is clear, however, that such global authorities hardly exist, and that, to the extent that they do, neither they nor the states on which they depend envisage their role in these terms. A programme of global responsibility requires the development of a new global consensus, but this can hardly be a consensus of states alone. Although it must work through the existing international institutions, and involve the transformation of those institutions, it must arise primarily through the development of global civil society.

This perspective can only be centred on a new unity of

purpose among Western peoples and governments, since only the West has the economic, political and military resources and the democratic and multinational institutions and culture necessary to undertake it. The West has a historic responsibility to take on this global leadership, not because it should impose itself on the rest of the world, but because so many people in the rest of the world look to it for support.

This perspective poses a particular challenge to the Western left. The left has long advocated intervention by the state in the national economy; it should now grasp the nettle of global intervention, and work out the programme of global responsibility, and the development of global institutions, around which such intervention should be formed. It is a curious anomaly that many radicals, who have little sympathy for laissez-faire as an economic principle within states, should uphold it so vigorously in international politics, often making a totem of the fact that the UN Charter specifically forbids any violation of national sovereignty. It is testimony to how far the left in its present defensive mode remains wedded to nationalism – whether home-grown or, in the case of the 'solidarity' left, that of others – rather than to genuine internationalism or globalism.

## Military intervention and the new wars

One of the reasons for resistance to the principle of global intervention is that it has been raised first and foremost in a military form. This is, however, an index of the weakness of international institutions and of their legitimacy. Like Western nation-states in the nineteenth century, late twentieth-century international organizations lack a developed capacity for surveillance and hence depend too much on military intervention. The answer is hardly to prevent international military interventions, but to elaborate the global political, economic and social mechanisms which make military action less necessary. In every case, the cost of effective political intervention to resolve crises short of war will represent an enormous saving, in financial as well as human terms, compared to the results of armed conflict.

When the Cold War ended and the Soviet Union collapsed, the mechanisms for such political interventions hardly existed and the political will and experience necessary for them were certainly not available in the great powers or in the United Nations. The crises generated a new wave of wars – the results of the breakdown of empires and alliances – of which only the first major test, in the Gulf, drew a major international military response. Subsequent wars, from Croatia and Bosnia to Armenia–Azerbaijan, Georgia and Moldova, to Cambodia, Somalia and Angola, have attracted varying levels of response, but all at a far lower level than that in the Gulf. The clear differentiation in the Gulf case is that there, uniquely, major United States and other Western economic and strategic interests were at stake.[1]

The Gulf War involved three major social crises: the terrorization of Kuwaiti society by Iraqi troops; the impoverishment of Iraqi society as a result of the Western destruction of its physical infrastructure, together with sanctions; and the decimation of Shia communities, and threatened genocide of the Kurds, in the aftermath of unsuccessful revolts inspired by the Iraqi defeat and Western propaganda. The international interventions overcame the hardship of Kuwaitis, although not of many non-Kuwaiti citizens (as a by-product of restoring the state); they also actually caused the impoverishment of Iraq, and finally responded partially and temporarily with 'safe havens' to the plight of the Kurds (but not of the Shias).

The unevennesses in response to the suffering of different groups of people in this context can stand as a sign of the current situation as a whole. The Western powers rescued the prosperous Kuwaitis but did little for their poor South Asian and Palestinian servants. They spared Iraqi civilians from deliberate, direct bombardment but exposed them to the effects of blowing up their water, sewage and electricity systems as well as to 'collateral damage' from attacks on 'military targets'. They ignored the plight of the Shias and, initially, the Kurds, but turned to protect the Kurds when they were extensively depicted in the global media – only to wind down their operations, leaving the Kurds surviving precariously, when media attention subsided.

What this balance sheet shows is clearly that the terms of military intervention were dictated primarily by the strategic and political interests of the powers involved, rather than any consistent concern to protect society. At the same time, society was at times protected, partly as a by-product of other interests, and partly because (in the Kurdish case) its survival itself became a political issue within Western states. The Kurdish case raised the fascinating spectre of 'humanitarian intervention' which has haunted subsequent crises.

These later crises have posed the relationships between humanitarianism and military action, and between Western state interests, international institutions, media and civil society, in even more acute forms. Western media have been relatively full in their coverage of Bosnia – but only in comparison with the almost total neglect has also been much more extensive in ex-Yugoslavia than in any of the other cases, but military intervention, much heralded, has been limited (at the time of writing) largely to the protection of humanitarian aid convoys. That protection has been interpreted, moreoever, in minimalist terms, not even entailing a determination to force a passage through Serbian and Croatian roadblocks. The UN-proclaimed 'safe havens' made a mockery even of the very limited concept applied in the Kurdish case, with no attempt until 1994 to halt the ceaseless bombardment of these areas.

In Bosnia, genocide has been carried out on a scale previously unimaginable in post-1945 Europe. International intervention was limited, for two years, to an attempt to mitigate the effects of genocide, not to prevent or halt it or undo its results. On the contrary, the mediation process has ratified the effects of the mass expulsions and killings of civilians. Bosnia was, by any standards, a dismal, indeed criminal, failure of the 'international community' to uphold its professed goals and values. It was not a failure of a military intervention carried out (as might be argued of Somalia in 1993), but a failure to intervene militarily when a discriminating use of military force might have protected hundreds of thousands of lives, saved multi-ethnic communities, and maintained a state which – despite undoubted weaknesses – was attempting to uphold pluralist and democratic principles.

The Bosnian case has been so critical, not because its European location makes it intrinsically more important than crises in the Caucasus, southern Africa or South-East Asia, but because the extent of media and political intervention has made it a test case. It has been a failure of global civil society as much as of the 'community' of states. No forces of sufficient strength have emerged in Western civil societies to connect the mediated violence of the war with a political will to protect Bosnian society. Old political parties and new social movements alike have failed to find effective means of connecting with the crisis. Successive mediated crises – the outbreak of war itself; the exposure of conditions in Serbian concentration camps; the siege of Srebrenica; 'Operation Irma' and the evacuation of wounded children from Sarajevo – failed to generate a decisive political impact, until the bombing of a Sarajevo market in February 1994.[2]

The reasons for these failures lie centrally in the narrow interpretation of Western strategic interests by the European powers and the United States. They have been magnified by governments' and media's projection of the Bosnian war as an 'inter-ethnic' conflict and the Bosnian government as just another 'ethnic' faction, together with the understandable lack of enthusiasm of people and governments for involvement in UN-authorized war against Serbian and Croatian forces which would entail Western casualties. In addition to these factors, there were undoubtedly military difficulties in any operation in Bosnia, particularly one on the ground which aimed to protect civilian populations threatened by Serbian and Croatian forces without causing large casualties among Serb and Croat civilians.

It is difficult to argue, however, that these constitute sufficient reasons for abstention from international military intervention. Even if there are not strong particular Western interests in ex-Yugoslavia of the kind which lay behind the intervention in the Gulf, there is a larger Western interest in global stability, and a particular Western European interest in wider European regional stability. If it was dangerous to allow Iraq's aggression against Kuwait to stand, so must it be to allow Serbia and Croatia to succeed against Bosnia. The incitement to others – Armenia, the Khmer Rouge, UNITA in Angola, and doubtless more to come – is obvious. Even at the narrow level of state interests, the Western powers may yet pay dearly for their and the UN's weakness in Bosnia.

In broader terms, the scale and the depths of the genocide in Bosnia represent the fundamental fragility of the integration of global society. They are basic affronts to the values upon which the West has claimed to base its post-Cold War reconstruction of the international order. They strike a very large blow at the 'European ideal' and account for a good deal of the pessimism which has surrounded the project of European integration in the 1990s. It is impossible to believe that military measures could not have been taken to relieve beseiged cities and towns and protect their inhabitants, and to lay the basis for a process – undoubtedly a long and difficult one, but necessary nonetheless – of restoring a democratic state respecting individual and minority rights of all kinds.

Bosnia has been a case – and there are undoubtedly others – where international military intervention would have been justified. Ideally, of course, adequate prior political intervention would have made military action unnecessary. In making a case for military intervention it is essential to underline that it should be seen in the context of the development of international intervention as a whole, not as a substitute for it. Every case of military intervention represents, at root, a failure of political and other forms of intervention. As global state action develops and becomes more sophisticated, military power should eventually become less fundamental as a means of that action.

In the short term, military intervention will undoubtedly be a major part of global state intervention, and the situations in which it used, the forms it takes, and its perceived success or failure will clearly be of major significance for the process as a whole. It is important to define the goals of this form of intervention: the simple goals of stability and peacekeeping must be balanced with the upholding of human rights and democracy and peacemaking. It is also necessary to define the criteria by which operations are formulated and assessed. Clarity of political purpose, organization and command must replace ideas of a quick military 'fix', such as have predominated in the US/UN operation in Somalia.

A fundamental issue is clearly the institutional structure for international intervention. The UN has become far more pivotal than many would have imagined at the beginning of the decade. It has clearly re-established some of its authority as the centre of legitimate international decision-making and intervention. It is obviously important than an institution-building process should take place in which the UN must have a central position, with adequate resources, reformed structures (although that is a large subject beyond the scope of this chapter) and greater authority *vis-à-vis* individual states. There should be a bias in favour of UN-authorized rather than freelance regional operations, and of UN-organized rather than sub-contracted operations. In this way the UN can itself be built up. At the same time, it must be recognized that the UN is not a global state, that there are very severe limitations on its power, and that in the short run it cannot but be dependent on the great powers.

The requirements of global institution-building must always be balanced, moreover, against those of effective action in a given situation. In the absence of permanent UN armed forces, it is inevitable that the UN will depend on states, and it is more important that action should be successful in protecting people than that it should be undertaken by particular institutions. In the absence of a global state, it is unavoidable that global state action will be undertaken largely by states, *ad hoc* coalitions of states and more permanent regional groupings of states acting in particular contexts. The pattern of global state intervention will be complex and messy, probably for decades to come. While we should do what we can to simplify and improve it, and make it more accountable to and legitimate in society, we cannot argue away the complexity.

The fact that global state action is undertaken by groups of states in which major Western powers – above all the sole surviving superpower, the USA – are dominant undoubtedly gives rise to particular difficulties. These states will certainly pursue their own interests, not act neutrally as agents or conduits of international power. The development of global institutions and intervention will therefore be coloured by these interests and may seem at times blatantly self-interested or partisan. There will undoubtedly be continuations, implicit and sometimes explicit, of historic colonialism and imperialism. These are unavoidable, given the realities of world power which dictate that the Western powers will provide the main basis for global state action. This does not mean, of course, that such distortions should simply be accepted, but that we should see the process of correcting them as a part of the process of developing international intervention, rather than finding in this factor a reason for rejecting intervention as such.

## Towards global responsibility

The development of global society requires a new politics of global responsibility. Our discussion has shown that we can hardly expect such a politics to come, well formed or consistently, out of the miasma of existing international institutions as they intersect with state interests. Such a politics requires us to address issues of global inequality, poverty and environmental stress, as well as of human rights, minority rights, democracy and individual and group security, which cut hugely across dominant interests on a world scale as well as within just about every state. A politics of global responsibility is overwhelmingly a politics which will find its basis in civil society, in the articulation of interests and solidarities, rather than directly in the arena of states. It is a politics which will be characterized, sometimes disparagingly, as utopian, although it is based, I hope to have demonstrated, on real trends and possibilities.

A major problem in developing such a politics in civil society is its necessarily double-edged relationship to the embryonic forms of global state power. The sorts of politics which work best in civil society, as the bases for social movements, are the simple and elemental politics based on strong positives – for humanitarian aid to the starving, for example – or negatives – such as the rejection of nuclear weapons. Such politics often assume, in practice, a simple relationship to the state: either demanding a change in policy, or rejecting a particular part of the state (for example, its nuclear arms and by implication its military activities as such) altogether.

A more developed, all-embracing politics of global responsibility cannot include such relatively simple positions. It has no alternative but to explore the tension between civil society and the state, and within state institutions at a national and global level, in a more complex way. It is not a statist politics, as it recognizes very fully the limitations of state action. It is, however, a politics which recognizes the necessity of state-building, of developing state activity, as well as of keeping this very much in balance with the needs of society.

In the rapidly global society, nation-states and other nationally based institutions are not outmoded, but change their functions and purposes. They monitor each other as well as the functioning of the growing number of global systems. In this sense, surveillance develops within global society as a process of mutual recognition by segmental bodies. At the same time, global systems require global monitoring and regulation, and global institutions develop accordingly. The late twentieth century has seen a proliferation of international organizations, regulating or coordinating different systems within the developing global economy and society. At the apex of this network are the global state institutions themselves, coordinating and increasingly regulating the system of states. Just as state institutions constitute the ultimate authoritive institutions within the national context, so global state institutions are beginning to be consolidated as the highest authoritive institutions on a world scale.

The paradox of the new global politics is that, given the reluctance of nation-states to cede authority upwards, global state-building needs the assistance of forces in civil society. The increasing authority and accountability of international institutions must go hand in hand, and they will be established only through an alliance of globally minded elements in state institutions (including international organizations) and globally minded forces within civil society.

The difficulty of this task is that the new global politics raises the most problematic forms of international intervention, such as military action. The Bosnian crisis can be seen as symbolic of this problem. The crisis brought together issues which have enormous popular resonance – resistance to racism and genocide, opposition to war and support for humanitarian relief – and yet it has been impossible to develop a strong popular consensus, or a social movement, largely because all these issues were deeply entangled with the issue of UN military intervention. As we have seen, there were powerful reasons why this option was blocked.

The issue of military intervention can hardly be avoided, however, and can be come to terms with only by developing a larger politics of global responsibility and intervention. This politics is now beginning to emerge, and will become an increasingly critical trend in the final years of the twentieth century. As nation-states – including the most powerful – turn in on themselves, with the collapse of Cold War rivalries and ideologies, the global crises of the new era are being posed with new force. The new politics is needed if these crises are to be answered and the world is to move forward.

## NOTES

1  The discussion of the Gulf and subsequent crises which follows is based on research which will be fully reported in my book *Distant Violence: Mediation and Civil Society in the New Crises of Global Society*, London: Frances Pinter, forthcoming.
2  I intend to examine these cases in detail in further research on the mediation of the Bosnian war.

# Index